PRAYING *for* GUIDANCE

HOW TO DISCOVER GOD'S WILL

RON KINCAID

InterVarsity Press
Downers Grove, Illinois

InterVarsity Press® is the book-publishing division of InterVarsity Christian Fellowship®, a student movement active on campus at hundreds of universities, colleges and schools of nursing in the United States of America, and a member movement of the International Fellowship of Evangelical Students. For information about local and regional activities, write Public Relations Dept., InterVarsity Christian Fellowship, 6400 Schroeder Rd., P.O. Box 7895, Madison, WI 53707-7895.

All Scripture quotations, unless otherwise indicated, are taken from the HOLY BIBLE, NEW INTERNATIONAL VERSION®. NIV®. Copyright ©1973, 1978, 1984 by International Bible Society. Used by permission of Zondervan Publishing House. All rights reserved.

Cover photograph: SuperStock

ISBN 0-8308-1689-5

Printed in the United States of America ♻

Library of Congress Cataloging-in-Publication Data

Kincaid, Ron
    Praying for guidance: how to discover God's will/Ron Kincaid.
       p.   cm.
    Includes bibliographical references,
    ISBN 0-8308-1689-5 (pbk.: alk. paper)
    1. Prayer—Christianity.   2. God—Will.   3. Christian life.
  I. Title.
  BV215.K485   1996   95-48960
  248.3'2—dc20   CIP

| 21 | 20 | 19 | 18 | 17 | 16 | 15 | 14 | 13 | 12 | 11 | 10 | 9 | 8 | 7 | 6 | 5 | 4 | 3 | 2 | 1 |
| 13 | 12 | 11 | 10 | 09 | 08 | 07 | 06 | 05 | 04 | 03 | 02 | 01 | 00 | 99 | 98 | 97 | 96 |

To all my brothers and sisters
in Christ
who seek to know and do God's will
and with special thanks to
my friend Mike Donahue
and my editor, Cindy Bunch-Hotaling,
who helped immensely
by reading
and editing my manuscript.

ONE

Finding Our Way out of the "Will-of-God Quagmire"

♦

ONE of my finest friends, a news anchorman in Portland, Oregon, was invited to Russia to do some news stories. Those issuing the invitation promised to secure an interview with President Yeltsin and make all the arrangements. Although obstacles appeared almost immediately, the opportunity beckoned. In spite of difficulties in putting together the trip, getting visas and making reservations, my friend persevered and made the trip.

He later confided to me that the trip raised questions for him about God's will. He wondered whether God had really wanted him to go on that trip. Initially he had thought it was God's will for him to go, but after encountering many problems he began to question if he had been following God's leading. For example, when he arrived in Moscow, nothing turned out as had been planned. The interview with

Yeltsin fell through. My friend was asked to make a sixteen-hour trip by car, during which the car was stopped and searched several times by the police. He found himself in situations that challenged his professional ethics. Then, as a result of the long hours of preparation and difficult travel, he got sick. On his return, he wondered whether the trip had been worth the trouble and cost—and whether it had been God's will for him to go at all.

There are few questions I am asked more frequently than "How can I know God's will for my life?" or "What does God want me to do in this situation?" or "Do you think I made the right decision?"

On a recent episode of a teen soap opera, a confused girl tried to choose between two boys. A friend took her hand and said, "When the time comes to make that decision, you'll know in your heart what's right for you." This is a Western mantra, our culture's creed when it comes to buying a car, picking a lifestyle or choosing a relationship. But for most people I know, the choices are not that clear-cut. Guidance seems murky.

All of us struggle at one time or another with questions about whether or not we made a good decision and whether what we did was really God's will for us. Everyone is troubled at times with major anxieties about the future: Where should I go to school? Whom should I marry? Which church should I attend? Should we have another child? Should I take that job, go to graduate school or volunteer overseas for a couple of years? Is God leading us to move to another state? Is the city a good place to raise a family? We all want to make wise choices, because decisions we make today determine our direction for tomorrow.

Occult Guidance

Many people are turning to astrologers and the occult for guidance. In years past astrologers operated in silence and kept their identity a secret. No longer. What was once practiced behind closed doors in sleazy quarters with shades drawn and was considered part hoax with a touch of superstitious hocus-pocus is now big business.

Did you know that there are now Wall Street astrologers? One is Arch Crawford, who warned of a "horrendous crash" after a market top "around August 24." He figured it on the basis of his study of the stars "when five planets formed a 'grand trine' with Jupiter." Remember the date of the actual top of the market? It was August 25, followed by "Black Monday" in October 1988.

Jeane Dixon, the world's leading astrologer and "voice of prophecy," writes a syndicated column that appears in 450 newspapers worldwide. She travels the globe speaking to large audiences that are consistently standing-room only. Sorcerers and astrologers are growing in popularity because people hunger to know the future.

How do Christians obtain guidance about their future? Some exhort us to seek a deep, mystical confirmation before deciding on a course of action. Others bid us read every circumstance in our lives as a sign from God. Still others say, "Use your brain. That's why God gave you one!" Where do we look for help?

Obstacles or Signs?

My wife, Jorie, is the director of Orphans Overseas, an all-volunteer adoption agency and orphan relief organization that currently is facilitating adoptions in Russia, China and Vietnam. It also does relief work in these countries, as well as in Romania and Albania. In addition to its international work, it carries out domestic adoptions.

Recently the staff did a study of the Portland area and found that many young women who were choosing abortions would have opted to keep their baby or put the child up for adoption if a birth-mom home had been available for them. So the board of directors of Orphans Overseas voted to purchase a home that could be converted into a birth-mom home.

During the process of seeking funding and purchasing a home, they ran into all kinds of obstacles. I found it fascinating to watch how different Christians reacted to obstacles that frustrated the purposes they believed God had put before them.

In the face of difficulties, some board members simply said, "We must keep praying." Others interpreted opposition as a signal that they were out of the will of God. One man, when faced with a delay, would say, "There's a check." A few days later, in the face of another setback, he would say, "There's another check." He interpreted difficulties as a sign from God that they should abort the project.

There's another way to look at problems. We could just as easily interpret obstacles as a sign that we should persevere. If the apostle Paul had interpreted the opposition he encountered as a sign that God did not want him to go forward with the message of Christ, he would have never taken the gospel to the Gentiles. More than likely he would have gone home with John Mark after they reached Perga. He would have stopped preaching after the Jewish leaders opposed them in Antioch in Pisidia, when the people in Iconium put together a plot to stone him or when the people of Lystra stoned him.

Problems need not be interpreted as evidence that we are out of the will of God. Jesus told us that believers would face opposition:

If the world hates you, keep in mind that it hated me first. If you belonged to the world, it would love you as its own. As it is, you do not belong to the world, but I have chosen you out of the world. That is why the world hates you. Remember the words I spoke to you: "No servant is greater than his master." If they persecuted me, they will persecute you also. If they obeyed my teaching, they will obey yours also. They will treat you this way because of my name, for they do not know the One who sent me. (Jn 15:18-21)

Many of the difficulties we face come as a result of our union with Christ.

Some Christians interpret difficult circumstances as a sign that we must have strayed from God's will for us. Others translate day-to-day circumstances as signals from God to direct us in our decision-making. Some time ago a Christian adoption facilitator called Jorie to say that a birth mom who was giving birth in a few weeks had rejected all the prospective adoptive parents in their files. She asked Jorie to rush over five files that she could show the birth mom. Jorie asked her staff to find five couples who would be interested in this new adoption possibility and quickly sent their files to this woman.

A couple days later the facilitator called back to report: "Just after I talked to you, a couple I had talked with months before who had never completed their paperwork called about the possibility of adopting. I believe God caused them to call at that moment because they were his choice to adopt the baby. So I had them put together a file. I decided not to show the birth mom the files you sent me after all. I'm certain it was God's will for this couple to adopt the baby, because the birth mom liked their file and chose them."

This serves as an example of strange ways people have of ascertaining God's will. The woman based her entire decision about God's will on a single circumstantial event. She knew next to nothing about this couple except that they called at just the right time. She overlooked other factors such as the interview, the application, the home study and the fact that others had turned in their files ahead of this couple. Orphans Overseas works very hard to place babies in homes in the order in which prospective parents complete their paperwork. This woman rejected typical placement protocol. Her decision-making process suggested that God's will bypasses all human reasoning. She wanted God to give her a sign that would take away all her freedom to make wise choices on her own.

Furthermore, showing the birth mom only the one file she decided was God's will and not showing the other files indicated that she didn't trust God's sovereignty. She apparently figured that God was not intelligent enough to choose the right family or not powerful enough to direct the birth mom to the best choice. So she helped God out by showing only the one file.

Why do many believers place so much emphasis on circumstances as a means of ascertaining God's will? Is there biblical basis for this? Why do many Christians interpret problems as a sign that God is against whatever it is they are doing? The derivation of this kind of thinking was prevalent in mainstream Christianity long before our time.

The Traditional Approach to Finding God's Will

The usual approach begins with the assumption that for each of our decisions God has one and only one correct choice he wants us to make. It assumes that God has a blueprint for each believer's life, such as getting married to one perfect person at age twenty-six, moving to Phoenix for fourteen years, going on to Cincinnati for twenty years and then retiring in Portland. The goal of the believer is to discover God's perfect plan and discern the one correct choice God has in each decision. I illustrate this approach in pictorial form in diagram 1.

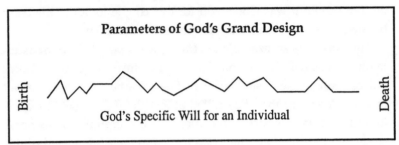

Diagram 1

The rectangle represents the parameters of God's grand design. The jagged line marks God's individual will for each believer. The duty of the believer, according to the usual approach to discerning God's will, is to find that "jagged line," God's individual plan for his or her life for each day. The process for determining God's will in each decision is to interpret the inner impressions and outward signs through which the Holy Spirit leads. The confirmation that we are correctly discerning God's leading comes from an inner sense of peace and outward successful results.

What happens when Christians marry the wrong partner, take the wrong job, refuse to accept God's call to be a missionary or bypass countless opportunities because of unbelief? Can they ever again prove that "good, pleasing and perfect will" of God? Must they resign themselves to settling for God's second best the rest of their lives?

Sometimes we get the impression that the will of God is like an egg, a heavenly Humpty-Dumpty. Presumably, God expects us to do a balancing act as we walk an invisible tightrope. One mistake—or, at the most, two—and no one, not even God, can put Humpty-Dumpty together again.

Problems with the Traditional Approach
I find the traditional approach to discerning God's will confusing and

unsatisfying. It leaves basic questions about God's sovereignty and grace unanswered. Specifically, there are five problems with the traditional approach to finding God's will unanswered.

The first problem is that *passages used to prove God's individual will for Christians have more to do with God's moral will for all believers.*[1] A discussion of God's will is murky unless we distinguish God's moral will from his individual will for believers. God's *moral will* is the sum of his commands revealed in the Bible about what to believe and how to live. God's *individual will* is a reference to God's detailed life-plan uniquely designed for each person, such as God's calling Jeremiah to be a prophet (Jer 1:5), his setting apart John the Baptist to prepare the way for the Lord (Lk 1:13-17) or his setting aside Paul to preach to the Gentiles (Gal 1:15-16).

Advocates of the traditional approach quote passages such as the following:

Be very careful, then, how you live—not as unwise but as wise, making the most of every opportunity, because the days are evil. Therefore do not be foolish, but understand what the Lord's will is. (Eph 5:15-17)

For this reason, since the day we heard about you, we have not stopped praying for you and asking God to fill you with the knowledge of his will through all spiritual wisdom and understanding. (Col 1:9)

They claim that these texts speak of God's specific directions for our lives. But Paul is talking about God's grand design that is the same for all believers. They may also cite Romans 12:1-2:

Therefore, I urge you, brothers, in view of God's mercy, to offer your bodies as living sacrifices, holy and pleasing to God—this is your spiritual act of worship. Do not conform any longer to the pattern of this world, but be transformed by the renewing of your mind. Then you will be able to test and approve what God's will is—his good, pleasing and perfect will.

The common interpretation is that, if we present our bodies a living sacrifice and renew our minds, then God will lead us to the precise individualized plans he has for us. However, Paul is not talking about God's individual will but his moral will. In fact, you cannot make a clear case from Scripture that God has a detailed blueprint for each Christian's life

Second, *the traditional approach serves as an attempt to take away our freedom.* When Christians plead with God to show them specific plans for their future, in many cases they are asking for something God is not pleased to give. They ask God to show them what to do, rather than to help them make responsible decisions.

When people come to counselors for advice, most just want someone to listen to them and help them sort through their thoughts. But others want to be told what to do. Such clients yearn for a wise parent to make all the important decisions. But a wise counselor refuses to play a parental role. The client needs to take the advice and develop the mature ability to make his or her own decisions.

The counselor's response offers an important insight concerning one of the most puzzling aspects of guidance. In reference to morally neutral issues—those not dealt with in Scripture—why doesn't God come right out and tell us which decision is the correct one? Could it be that such a response would inevitably jeopardize human freedom? Some Christians want a relationship in which God tells them what to do. Then they wonder why his guidance is so much less clear than a lawyer's or a doctor's.

I believe that God refrains from making everything about the future clear to us because he knows we would have no meaningful opportunity for faith or obedience. If we knew the inevitable result of taking one sort of action and not another, human freedom would dissolve. God gives us freedom. Just as it means nothing when a woman tells a man she loves him while he is holding a gun to her head, God knows that true love can only be offered voluntarily. So he gives us freedom to accept or reject, obey or disobey him.

It is ironic that throughout history we Christians have found ourselves praying for specific guidance that would have the effect of taking away our freedom. But God has no intention of doing that. Many believers pray for signs, like Gideon's fleece, far too often. They are asking God to take away their freedom, a request that God will not grant. God desires not so much to run our lives as to have us offer our lives to him in obedience.

Hannah Whitall Smith tells of a woman who each morning, having consecrated the day to the Lord as soon as she awoke, "would then ask him whether she was to get up or not," and would not stir until "the voice" told her to dress. "As she put on each article she asked the Lord whether she was to put it on, and very often the Lord would tell her to put on the right shoe and leave off the other; sometimes she was to put on both stockings and no shoes; and sometimes both shoes and no stockings; it was the same with all the articles of dress."[2] The woman wanted God to take away all her freedom so that she did not have to take responsibility for her own decisions.

A third problem with the traditional approach to finding God's will is that *it is of little use in the everyday decisions of life.* I don't know any Christians who claim absolute assurance in knowing God's individual will for them in decisions such as which clothes they wear to work, which route they take to the store, where they sit in church and what they eat for dinner. Hardly anybody I know struggles over whether God wants them to cook green beans or snow peas for dinner. They cook whatever seems best. They abandon the one-and-only-correct-choice paradigm when it comes to minor decisions. Virtually all Christians habitually make these decisions on the basis of what seems best to them at the time. That means they relegate finding God's perfect will only to the "presidential decisions."

A fourth inadequacy of the typical approach to finding God's will is that *it tends to promote immaturity in decision-making.* In relating several true stories of Christians who were trying to ascertain the will of God, I want to make sure I am not misunderstood. I am not attempting to ridicule or poke fun at people who pray for God to show them some kind of sign as to what they should do. I frequently make specific requests of God to help me determine what I should do. I am not suggesting that God never shows us signs to guide us. I do not even begin to suggest that the "peace of God, which transcends all [human] understanding" is unimportant in the process of making decisions. I simply want to raise the question: Is this a mature approach to decision-making? You be the judge.

Consider the experience of Tim Stafford, a writer whose advice is frequently sought by young people who are "obsessed with finding the right one." "I just got a letter last week," he said recently, "from a young woman who had seen tennis star Andre Agassi on TV and prayed that the Lord would confirm her impression that he was the one for her by showing her a Nevada license plate. Lo and behold, several Nevada license plates appeared."[3] Specific guidance or immaturity?

A woman received a brochure advertising a tour to Israel. Going to the Holy Land was one of her lifelong dreams. She had the money, the time and the interest. But was it God's will? Before going to bed one night she read the pamphlet once more and noticed that the airplane the group would be traveling on was a 747 jumbo jet. After spending a sleepless night wrestling with all the pros and cons, she was greatly relieved the following morning. She now knew it was God's will for her to go. How did she know? When she awoke and glanced at her digital clock, it read 7:47. That was her "sign" from God.[4] She was certain that she was now making the right decision because she had a sense of peace about it.

This "sense of peace" as the certain evidence of God's will has become an inside joke on our church staff. A couple years ago I shared some principles with our congregation about ascertaining God's will. I told them that typical teaching about obtaining guidance often amounts to little more than interpreting circumstantial signs and feeling a sense of peace about a decision. So when one of our pastoral staff members presents a plan he or she is trying to get the other pastors to agree to, the concluding statement is often "I feel a sense of peace about it."

The sad thing is that this kind of decision-making passes for deep spirituality in many evangelical Christian circles. Christians can use ridiculous methods for determining God's will, at the same time claiming to be tuned in to the frequency of the Spirit of God. Claiming that they are waiting on God's leading moment by moment, they adopt a "Who knows where I'll be next?" attitude as an indication that they are "in tune with God." Such thinking leads to spiritualizing irresponsibility or undependability, allowing a person to explain any late arrival, unpaid bill, neglected duty or overlooked obligation with the words "The Holy Spirit seemed to be leading me." Scripture, however, breathes a consistency between spirituality and dependability. Dependable believers don't blame God for their mistakes and immaturities.

Still a fifth inadequacy in the traditional approach to finding God's will is that *it tends to promote anxiety over missing God's one-and-only will rather than gratitude for multiple opportunities.* Some Christians have a terrible time making decisions because they live in fear of making the wrong choice and missing out on God's best for the rest of their lives.

We cannot substantiate from Scripture the commonly held notion that for every decision we make God has one and only one right choice for us. Furthermore, this teaching causes Christians a massive amount of undue stress and can cause them to make some foolish choices when making decisions. In something as important as decision-making, I want to make certain we really examine what the Bible teaches and bring our practice in line with the clear teaching of Holy Writ.

The Last Word

Is there a better approach to decision-making? Yes, there is. Scripture instructs us that instead of struggling to find the one and only right choice and God's blueprint for our lives, we should simply seek to make wise choices. Within God's grand design we are free to make choices. Thus in diagram 1 we're free to move about the rectangle without having to search for the jagged line.

We must always seek to obey God's moral will as revealed in Scripture. As long as we are living in obedience to Christ, we have freedom to make one of any number of choices. As Ted Engstrom says, "A Christian is the only person I know who can choose any one of four different directions and have it be right!" The question we ask when faced with a decision is not, What is God's specific individual will for me that I don't want to miss? but, What would be the prudent thing to do? or, What choice would bring Christ the most honor? Chapter two will present seven biblical principles for wise decision-making to help you in the process of learning to choose wisely.

Questions for Reflection and Discussion

1. How have you approached decision-making incorrectly?

2. Can you cite examples of Christians who made decisions they felt were in God's will but which you think may have been poor decisions because they employed immature approaches to decision-making?

3. Do you think some believers prefer a belief that God spells out his will for us in each decision to being given freedom to make decisions within the boundaries of God's grand design? Why or why not?

4. Read Romans 8:28-30. According to these verses, what is God's grand design for us?

5. What principle or insight was most helpful to you in chapter one?

TWO

Praying to Become Wise in Decision-Making

♦

SUPPOSE a friend of yours who graduated from college, works at a good job and is involved in ministry at her church tells you she is wondering about going back to graduate school or serving on an overseas mission field for a couple of years. She asks God to give her a sign so that she can know his will for her. That very week a friend calls and invites her to come live with her at graduate school. She decides God must be leading her to attend graduate school. But she has nagging doubts about whether she used a good method for determining God's will.

How would you counsel her? Is praying for a sign the best way to make wise decisions, or does it lead to immaturity in decision-making?

As we saw, the assumption that for every choice Christians make there is one and only one right decision if they are to remain in God's perfect will can lead to all kinds of difficulties. So this chapter introduces seven principles that form the foundation of a more biblical approach to praying for guidance.

Seek to Understand and Obey God's Grand Design

God's grand design is his revealed will for all humanity as laid out for us in the Scriptures. God's grand design is probably nowhere stated more succinctly than by the apostle Paul: "And we know that in all things God works for the good of those who love him, who have been called according to his purpose. For those God foreknew he also predestined to be conformed to the likeness of his Son, that he might be the firstborn among many brothers" (Rom 8:28-29). These verses tell us that God has a purpose, a plan. God decided beforehand that his will for us is threefold: to know Christ, to be conformed to the likeness of Christ and to share Christ.

Those whom "God foreknew" are those he called into a relationship with himself through Christ. Paul writes to Timothy, "This . . . pleases God our Savior, who wants all men to be saved and to come to a knowledge of the truth" (1 Tim 2:3-4). Jesus says in John 6:40, "For my Father's will is that everyone who looks to the Son and believes in him shall have eternal life." *God's grand design is, first of all, that we come to faith in Christ.*

It is also God's grand design that we "be conformed to the likeness of his Son" (Rom 8:29). Paul writes in 1 Thessalonians 4:3, "It is God's will that you should be sanctified: that you should avoid sexual immorality." We are called to become pure like Christ is pure. Christ tells us that he came to fulfill the law (Mt 5:17). Jesus Christ's life represented the perfect fulfillment of the commandments. So when we seek to obey the Ten Commandments, which are written on our hearts when we give our lives to Christ, we are fulfilling God's grand design.

Since God wants to conform us to the likeness of Christ, he can utilize practically any event or circumstance in our lives as a springboard to this process. In this sense, God's will may not be so much people and places as the *process* of us growing to maturity in Christ. That is why Paul is able to say that "in all things God works for the good of those who love him" (Rom 8:28). If we respond to life's experiences properly, God can use any problems that come our way to conform us into the likeness of his Son.

The third part to God's grand design is that we share Christ with others. Christ called us to be adopted as God's children and to be conformed to his likeness so "that he might be the firstborn among many brothers" (Rom 8:29). If Christ is to be the first among many brothers, we must spread the news of God's grace so that others become part of God's family as well.

Some of Jesus' final words to his disciples were "Go and make disciples of all nations, baptizing them in the name of the Father and of the Son and of the Holy Spirit, and teaching them to obey everything I have commanded you" (Mt 28:19-20). God's grand design is not just that we come to know Christ and become like Christ; he also wants us to share the message of Christ with others.

The key to seeking God's guidance is to know the grand design. When I know that God's grand design for me is to know Christ, become like Christ and become a blessing to the world, I make better decisions about the stewardship of my time, talents, gifts, money and relationships.

My wife, Jorie, tells me that once she discovered this principle of decision-making she felt release from a great deal of guilt and worry about making wrong choices. Rather than being anxious about every decision, she learned she could relax in Christ, knowing that she could make one of any number of choices and still be in God's will.

Many people have come to me for counsel concerning their selection of a mate: "Do you think he is the right one for me? Do you think I am making a mistake? I don't want to miss God's will for my life in the selection of a mate." Inherent in their questions lies the assumption that God has one and only one person for them to marry.

Although you will probably not find Bible verses that lead you to only one mate, you will find principles to guide you in the selection of a mate. The first and most important thing to look for is spiritual compatibility. If the person we choose to marry helps us fulfill God's grand design to know Christ, to be conformed to Christ and to share Christ, we are in God's will. If the person will not help us fulfill God's grand design, then he or she is not a good choice.

In 1 Corinthians 7:39 Paul writes, "A woman is bound to her husband as long as he lives. But if her husband dies, she is free to marry anyone she wishes [notice the freedom], but he must belong to the Lord." He must be a fellow believer. Paul also writes, "Do not be yoked together with unbelievers. For . . . what fellowship can light have with darkness?" (2 Cor 6:14). This is the most disliked sentence in all of Scripture for single people who are anxious to get married. It is a terrible verse if you're worried about getting married, for in one verse, Paul, under the inspiration of the Holy Spirit, cuts down the field from hundreds of thousands of marriageable candidates to really only a handful.

Suppose I'm trying to decide whether to be a lawyer, doctor, teacher or minister. According to the design, I don't ask God to show me if I should be a teacher. I ask him to conform me to Christ that I might be part of his grand design to bless the world. He leaves the decision of my occupation up to me. That explains why Scripture says very little about specific instructions God has for your life. God shows you the grand design and then says, "Now get on with your life." He says, "You decide whether to be a carpenter or an engineer, a musician or a computer programmer."

You say, "I'm waiting for God to show me what he wants me to do." God responds, "I've already told you enough. Love my Son, be conformed to my Son and share my love. Now you decide whether to be a pastor, a professional athlete or a plumber. That's your decision." God wants you to discover Christ's love, be changed by his love and then love the world. God cares deeply about you and what you do, but he won't take away your freedom.

Possibly you're wondering, "If I am free to choose whom to marry or what vocation to pursue, does that mean God has no individualized plans for me?" No. God called Abraham to be the father of many nations. He chose John the Baptist before he was even born to prepare the way for the Lord. He picked Simon and Andrew and James and John to be his disciples. He ordained Paul to preach the gospel to the Gentiles. He has planted within you specific passions, interests and abilities. He has granted you spiritual gifts to utilize in his service. He has some wonderful ways he would like to use you for his glory. But he will never present these desires that he has for you in a way that takes away your freedom. He wants you to discover your gifts and passions and choose how you will fulfill his grand design.

Perhaps an uneasy feeling is gnawing at you that wisdom guidance seems far less personal than the traditional view of God's will. You sense that if God gives you freedom to become a teacher, doctor or minister and you can fulfill his grand design no matter where you live, then God doesn't really care what choices you make. You feel like God is cut out of the decision-making process, and you are left with an impassive, deistic God.

Although I understand your fear, I do not share your concern. Nor did the apostles regard this approach as impersonal. They would agree that the wisdom approach to decision-making found in the New Testament is far less specific than the type of guidance we find in the Old Testament. God's guidance for the people of Israel focused on details: which persons were to be their spiritual leaders; exactly where they were to camp; how far they were to travel each day; when they were required to go to Jerusalem; which foods they could and could not eat; when they were to go to battle as a nation; when they must bathe; how much offering to give as a minimum; the exact dimensions of the tabernacle/temple; what uniforms the religious leaders must wear; and when male Israelites must be circumcised.

God's provisions for guidance in the New Testament, after the coming of Christ, are of a different character. Most of the specific regulations that constituted God's moral will for the Israelites have been moved into the area of freedom for Christians. We are free and responsible to decide for ourselves what to eat, what to wear, where we will live, which church we will attend and so on. And all decisions are to be governed by the general commands that make up God's grand design. The inescapable conclusion is this: "less specific" does not equal "less personal." God's method of guidance for Christians in the New Testament, though less specific than that given to Israel, is exactly suited to our status as children of God. If anything, we are closer to God, for now his Holy Spirit dwells within us, and we call God "Abba Father."

As his sons and daughters, we are given more freedom to make decisions on our own, but that does not mean God has withdrawn from us and cares less about us, does it? No. In his wisdom, God saw fit to guide Old Testament saints as "immature children" who had a limited understanding of his will. But those who have the benefit of receiving the revelation of Jesus Christ and the empowerment of his Spirit, God treats as "grown-up children." New Testament believers are equipped to relate to their Father on an "adult" level without requiring the detailed parental supervision that was appropriate to childhood.

The fact that God guides Christians as a father guides his children is proof of his personal concern for us. It is the same with our own sons and daughters. When our oldest son was young, Jorie and I made practically every decision for him. We decided what he would wear, what he would eat and how much, what time he would go to bed and when he was allowed to get up again. Now that he is seventeen, he makes most decisions for himself. He knows our family values. He recognizes the grand design we have for all our kids. Now we relate to him primarily on an adult level.

Does this mean we are any less personal with him? When we refuse to make decisions for him, does it mean we care about him less? Of course not. At times we have to bite our tongues to keep from offering advice or giving directions. But we know we are better parents if we allow him the freedom to make decisions for himself. By refraining from telling him what to do, we are showing him more love, not less.

This helps us better understand God's guidance for us. If we grant that in this New Testament age God gives us more freedom to make our own decisions about what is best, it does not mean he loves us any less. He may not lead us to find the one and only right path to take in each situation, but he leads us personally so that we learn to make wise choices.

Enjoy the Freedom God Has Given You to Make Wise Choices

I appreciate the freedom God has given me to think and reason and make choices within the parameters of his grand design. It has not made God impersonal at all. In fact, I can't imagine how my relationship with Christ could become any more personal.

God has given us freedom. The New Testament is very clear on this.

God does not take away your freedom in faith, and he does not take away your freedom in other choices. It is silly to ask God for guidance in areas where he has given us freedom.

Suppose a mountain has five routes to the top. It is foolish to insist on one and only one route when all five routes are adequate. Some people get bogged down in decision-making when they do not need to. What job should I take? That's your decision. Where should I live? That's your decision. Where should I minister? That's your decision.

I do not mean to imply that God is not interested in these decisions. He loves you and wants to be involved in all your decisions. Most times, however, he guides you in subtle ways. He feeds ideas into your mind, speaks through a nagging sensation of dissatisfaction, brings to the surface hidden dangers of temptation and perhaps even re-arranges certain circumstances. God's guidance will supply real help—but in ways that will not overwhelm your freedom.

One morning I came downstairs and found four-year-old Mark and two-year-old Andrea, who are great little friends, watching TV. They know they are not allowed to turn on the TV without our permission. They were also eating in the family room, another no-no. Andrea had four half-eaten, juicy, sticky peaches lying on the couch beside her and a full jar of raspberry jam on her lap that she was gleefully scooping into her mouth, although it looked like most of it had landed on her face and pajamas. Mark was sitting in a pile of prune pits, with a jar of Miracle Whip salad dressing he had spread all over the coffee table and was now greedily spooning into his mouth. When they saw the reaction on my face, they knew they had not chosen a wise course of action. In their freedom, they had not made a wise choice. God gives us freedom because he knows that we grow best when we are allowed to make choices.

After World War II Cardinal Cardine of Belgium looked around his country. It had been devastated. Every army in World War II, either advancing or retreating, had gone through Belgium. They had all left their footprints. He wondered what he could do to rebuild his country, so he set out walking to look around. Finding a large number of eleven- to thirteen-year-old orphans in his city, he got them together and said, "I will give you food and shelter. You can live with me, but on this condition: you must in return help to rebuild Belgium. I'll give you some time to decide and come back to see what your answer is."

When he came back, they said to him, "Yes, we will live with you, but what does it mean? How shall we rebuild our country?"

The cardinal replied, "I won't tell you what to do, but I'll give you a plan to decide what you should do. I'll teach you to pray. I'll read the Bible to you and help you meditate on God's Word. You'll learn to meditate and pray, and then you will find what God wants you to do, but I won't tell you what to do. You must decide what you can do to rebuild our country."

Here is the planning model he gave them. Step one: *See.* They were to look at the city, walk around and see what the needs were. Step two: *Judge.* They were to evaluate what was the most pressing need—what was the need they could meet. They were to ask God what they should do. Step three: *Act.* They would go and work their plan.

The orphans looked around the city and made their evaluation. They found that there were many other homeless orphans around the city and that soon it would be winter. They decided they would build little houses for them. So Cardinal Cardine gave them nails and hammers and showed them how to build serviceable houses that were little more than shacks.

When they completed the houses, they helped the orphans move in. Then they realized they needed to provide food. "What shall we do?" they asked.

The cardinal said, "I don't know, but I'll pray for you daily." The orphans decided they would give away half of the food that the cardinal gave them.

From that initial group of orphans who worked with Cardinal Cardine came the Christian Youth Workers' Movement, which has housed thousands of orphans throughout Europe. Many times the cardinal must have been tempted to tell them what to do, but instead he made them decide. He gave them the tools.

This teaching paradigm is similar to the way God deals with us. He gives us freedom to make choices within the parameters of his grand design. He gives us the tools we need to make good decisions: his Word, the Holy Spirit, prayer, good minds and wise counselors. But he doesn't take away our freedom.

We can make plans, but we must always humbly submit to God's sovereign plan, which may differ from our plans. When we pray, we should ask God to guide us in decisions that bring him honor and help fulfill his sovereign plan. James speaks to this issue:

Now listen, you who say, "Today or tomorrow we will go to this or that city, spend a year there, carry on business and make money." Why, you do not even know what will happen tomorrow. What is your life? You are a mist that appears for a little while and then vanishes. Instead you ought to say, "If it is the Lord's will, we will live and do this or that." (Jas 4:13-15)

James has no complaint about planning as such. It is the godless, self-assured attitude that he deplores. Believers are to adopt a humble attitude in planning. We recognize, as we plan, that no plan, whether good or bad, comes to pass unless God sovereignly wills it.

Commit Yourself Wholeheartedly to Doing God's Will

When we truly understand Jesus' words that he is the vine and we are the branches and that only if we remain in him can we bear much fruit (Jn 15:5), we recognize that without him we can know nothing but failure. We admit that on our own we make poor choices. This leads to total surrender to his will. We can all do at least one simple thing: place the helm of our lives, as sincerely as possible, in God's hands, entrust the direction of our lives to him, confess to him our inability to direct them for ourselves and ask him to direct them himself.

One of the great New Testament texts on guidance ends, "so that you may know what the will of God is." Paul begins this classic text, "I urge you, brothers, in view of God's mercy, to offer your bodies as living sacrifices, holy and pleasing to God" (Rom 12:1). This principle of wise decision-making is that you must give your life wholeheartedly to God. After all the mercy Christ extended to you, you should give yourself as a sacrifice to God. You say, "I'm yours, Lord. I'll do anything you want, go anywhere you want and be anything you want." That makes sense. Why should God waste his time helping you understand more of his grand design and the specific plans he has for your life if you show no interest in obeying that which he has already revealed to you? Why give you further direction when you're not committed to obeying what he has already shown you?

When God says, "Will you do my will?" our typical response is "Lord, tell me what it is so that I can decide." But when God sees that we have given our lives unreservedly to him, he can give us a deeper understanding of his will. It is necessary to point out, however, that this submitting of the will does not include a relinquishing of your brain. Some Christians want a relationship with God in which he tells them what to do moment by moment, and they no longer need to think or plan. Yielding your will to God entails a commitment to doing whatever he reveals to you through his Word or prayer. It does not mean that you do not need to use the mind God has given you.

Surrendering to God does not imply that we will be so surely guided by God that we will avoid all uncertainty, obscurity and anxiety in the search to know his will. Quite the contrary. The more we surrender to God, the more trouble we take to find out what God wants—studying the Scriptures, listening for his voice in prayer and being more severe than ever with ourselves in tracking down the sin that makes us impermeable to his inspiration. We must use our minds more keenly than ever to ensure that we are fulfilling God's grand design.

Renew Your Mind

Paul continues, "Do not conform any longer to the pattern of this world" (Rom 12:2). To obey God's grand design is to live in a way that does not conform to the standards of this world. It means to live in a way that brings honor to Jesus Christ.

A friend comes to you for advice. He has a well-paying job that he enjoys. He and his wife found Christ through the church and love their church. Their three children go to fine schools, are blessed with excellent friends and are involved in church activities. The problem is that he has been offered a much better-paying job in another city. He asks you if you think it is God's will for them to move. How would you counsel him?

The important question to get your friend to grapple with is his motives for moving. Does he believe he can bring more honor to Christ in another city and that a move would be better for his marriage and family? Or is he moving solely due to the lure of more money? Does his motivation for moving suggest that he is more conformed to the world or more conformed to Christ? Is he living by the world's standards or by obedience to God's grand design?

Paul resumes, "Be transformed by the renewing of your mind. Then you will be able to test and approve what God's will is—his good, pleasing and perfect will" (Rom 12:2). The Greek word *dokimazō* means "to prove" or "discern by testing." Paul says that if you renew your mind, you will discern and want to obey God's moral will. What is God's moral will? That we know Christ, become conformed to Christ and share Christ. That we be holy as God is holy (1 Pet 1:16). That we exhibit the fruit of the Spirit—love, joy, peace, patience, kindness, goodness, faithfulness, gentleness and self-control (Gal 5:22-23). That we make disciples of all nations (Mt 28:19). That we obey God's instructions clearly laid out for us in Scripture. When we renew our minds, we begin to think like God thinks and want to do what God wants. Since we know God's will, we will not delude ourselves into thinking we can do something that violates Scripture yet still bring honor to Christ.

The human mind is capable of convincing itself of anything in order to have its own way. Perhaps the most striking example of this self-delusion occurred with a young couple who decided to engage in sexual intercourse before marriage. Since the young man and woman had both been reared in the church, they had to find a way to lessen the guilt of this forbidden act. So they actually got down on their knees and prayed about what they were going to do, and they received "assurance" that it was all right to continue.[1]

How do we renew our minds? By studying and memorizing God's Word. By being regular in our worship attendance. By getting involved in small group Bible studies and accountability groups. By listening to God when we pray.

Trust God for the Wisdom to Make Good Decisions

When no specific guidance from God seems to be forthcoming, assume that he has already given you enough wisdom to make a good decision. James writes, "If any of you lacks wisdom, he should ask

God, who gives generously to all without finding fault" (Jas 1:5) or making us feel foolish or guilty. When you ask God for wisdom in some decision and no particular guidance seems to come, don't assume that God's Word is not true or that God fails to keep his promises. It could be that God, in his silence, is saying, "I've already given you all the wisdom you need to make a good decision. I've given you the tools; now you figure it out for yourself."

If you've asked God for wisdom, then he's given it to you, whether you feel wise or not. While you are waiting for God to give you more direction, God may be saying, "I've already given you all the guidance you need. I've given you my Word, a good mind and trusted friends. I've told you my grand design. Now you decide what you should do."

Thomas Bertram Costain, in his classic *The Silver Chalice*, creates a scene wherein Luke and his friends are looking for the sacred cup:

"We cannot walk blindly to the one place within these walls where it could rest safely, not unless the Lord directs us; and I do not yet hear the inner Voice that sometimes tells me what I am to say or do. Must we find the solution ourselves?" He went down on his knees and began to pray, "O Lord, look down upon us. We do not know which way to turn in this difficulty. Tell us how we may keep this sacred Cup from falling into wicked hands." After a moment of silence, he rose from his knees, "If the Voice does not speak to me now," he said, "we will know that for some reason we are expected to find the answer ourselves."[2]

Silence from heaven does not mean that God is not interested in leading us. More than likely it means that God has already given us enough guidance, and we are expected to make wise decisions with the information we already have.

Suppose you have been asked to serve as an elder, deacon or lay pastor in your church. You ask God to give you some clear indication as to what he wants you to do. But no specific guidance comes to you. God could be saying, "That's your decision. You decide if this would be a good use of your gifts and if this would be a good time for you to serve in this capacity."

In areas where the Bible gives no command, you are free to choose the course of action that best helps you fulfill God's grand design. The Bible doesn't give a lot of direction about many of the specific choices you need to make in life. Its silence suggests that God gives you freedom to choose the path that seems best. You can choose one of any number of careers or live in any number of places and still be in God's will.

A careful study of the New Testament shows that the early believers did not waste time trying to discern God's one-and-only correct choice in each situation. In areas where Scripture gave no special instructions, they simply did what seemed wise or most expedient. Look at some texts that illustrate New Testament decision-making:

□ Acts 17:7-15: The gospel brought about riots in Thessalonica, "so Paul moved to Berea."

□ 1 Thessalonians 3:1-2: Paul and Luke thought it best to remain in Athens and send Timothy to Thessalonica.

□ Philippians 2:25-26: Paul thought it necessary to send Epaphroditus to Philippi.

□ 1 Corinthians 16:3-4: Paul determined that if it was advisable, he would go to Jerusalem. He did what was prudent.

□ Acts 6:2-4: The apostles decided that it would not be right to neglect the ministry of the Word to wait on tables.

□ Acts 15:22, 25, 28: It seemed good not to burden the Gentiles with unnecessary regulations. They decided what regulations were essential.

□ Acts 19:21: Paul decided to go to Jerusalem. No all-night prayer sessions crying out for God's will—he simply decided to go.

□ Acts 21:4-5: Though the disciples at Tyre, led by the Holy Spirit, urged Paul not to go to Jerusalem, Paul stayed his course to Jerusalem. The Holy Spirit's counsel is not intended to take away our freedom. We are expected to use our minds and make good decisions.

In each of these texts we see that the early believers did what seemed most sensible. They made wise decisions on the basis of spiritual expediency. They tried to exercise good judgment without wasting time searching for the "one right choice." They showed maturity in their decision-making by basing their decisions on sound reasons.

I sense your question: "If God doesn't have a particular plan for us, then why pray?" Does the wisdom paradigm imply that we no longer need to ask for guidance? Not at all. James writes, "You want something but don't get it. You kill and covet, but you cannot have what you want. You quarrel and fight. You do not have, because you do not ask God" (Jas 4:2). The clear implication is that we are to ask. The apostle Paul counsels us to pray about everything (Phil 4:6). We are still to pray to God for guidance. We are short-sighted and confused human beings who need God's omniscient direction.

To say that we can choose one of any number of occupations is not to say that a particular one might not be better for you. To say that we are free to live wherever you want is not to say that one certain place might not be better. To say that we can choose one of any number of people to marry is not to say that one might not be better. We need God's direction so that we make wise choices. We do not pray for God to show us the one and only path but to guide us to make prudent choices.

Discovering that I can make one of any number of choices and still be in God's will has not caused me to pray less. I still try to talk to God about everything I do. I know the limitations of my wisdom and that my understanding is often darkened, so I seek his counsel. I engage with God in a nonstop conversation all through the day. I tell him what I am thinking. I ask him for wisdom in what I say during my appointments and for discernment as to people's deepest needs. Freedom to make choices does not reduce our need to ask God for guidance.

Get On with the Business of Living for Christ

Some people live in fear that they will make a wrong choice and miss God's perfect plan for their life. As long as you obey God's general moral will clearly laid out in Scripture, God gives you freedom to make choices that seem wise. Even when you make poor choices, God is big enough to overcome these foolish choices and bring you back in line with his grand design.

The notion that God has one specific plan for your life and that if you blow a choice you are relegated to God's second-best for the rest of your life shifts sovereignty from Creator to created. This means that I can, by my disobedience, force God to fall back to a second or third line of action, leaving him to maneuver within whatever leeway I have left him. Such thinking doesn't square with the apostle's encouraging word: "In all things God works for the good of those who love him."

John Mark made a poor choice to desert Paul and Barnabas on their first missionary journey. Was he cut from God's team for the rest of his life? No. Barnabas took him along on his next missionary tour. God used the acrimony between Paul and Barnabas as a means of forming two missionary teams. Years later, reconciliation took place between Paul and Mark. In some of the last words that flowed from the apostle's pen, Paul told Timothy to "get Mark and bring him with you, because he is helpful to me in my ministry" (2 Tim 4:11). Mark's desertion of Paul did not mean that he was banished from God's perfect will for the rest of his life. God still had big plans for him. And so did the apostle Paul.

David sinned by committing adultery with Bathsheba. Was he forever relegated to God's trash heap of moral failures? No. Through David's marriage with Bathsheba, God brought forth Solomon, the wisest king in Israel's history. The New Testament informs us that Jesus Christ traces his lineage back to Solomon and the marriage of David and Bathsheba.

All of this says to me, love God, relax and get on with the business of living! The good news is that God is sovereign over not only my life and my good choices but also my bad choices. That liberates me to live with assurance instead of with an apprehension that I may blow it.

Take Responsibility for Your Decisions

I believe that some Christians embrace traditional teaching about discerning the will of God so that they will not have to take responsibility for their decisions. If believers can convince others that God told them to do such-and-such or that he sent a circumstantial sign to guide them, then they can blame God for the negative outcome. They find it easier to say "It is God's will" than to accept the responsibility for their own decisions.

But if you want to grow wise in decision-making, you will take responsibility for your choices. When you make a bad decision, you will not blame it on God and deny your freedom but own up to the fact that it was your decision. Don't try to cloak your decisions with pious words such as "God told me to do this" or "God showed me I should do that," hoping to convince people that God has given you no choice in a certain matter. Scripture is clear that God does not take away your freedom. He will lead you and guide you, but he will never overpower your decision-making.

I know a Christian woman who used to attribute many of her decisions to God. One time I drew her aside and suggested that when she said "God told me to do this or that," she was inadvertently pulling a spiritual trump card on other people. After all, if God told her to do something, who was going to argue with God? She had created an airtight defense around all her statements and decisions. Furthermore, in the process she was not really taking responsibility for her decisions. She was not admitting that a course of action was really her decision—that God didn't do it, she did.

The Last Word

To become wise in decision-making, we will continue to seek God's guidance as we make decisions. We will still seek to depend on Christ moment by moment, for as Christ said, "Apart from me you can do nothing" (Jn 15:5). But when we ask God for guidance, it will not be to know his one-and-only right choice for us to make. Rather, it will be for God to help us make wise choices. We will ask, "Which decision will best help me know Christ, be conformed to Christ and share Christ?" Or we might ask, "Which choice will bring the most glory to Christ?" We will not ask God to overwhelm us with evidence, so as to take away our freedom. We will ask him to help us develop keen discernment so that we make God-honoring decisions.

I cannot help but think that this whole issue of divine guidance, which draws throngs of people to seminars and sells thousands of books, is overrated. God simply wants us to pray to know Christ, to be conformed to Christ, to share Christ with others and to make decisions that seem best in helping us to fulfill his grand design. Pray that way, and I assure you that you will become increasingly wise in decision-making.

Questions for Reflection and Discussion

1. According to chapter two, what is God's grand design for all

believers?

2 Do you believe that the wisdom paradigm for understanding God's will makes God less personal? Why or why not?

3. Why do you think we must commit ourselves wholeheartedly to God before we can expect to grow in our understanding of God's will?

4. Read Romans 12:1-2. What are some ways we can renew our minds so that we are more knowledgeable of God's grand design for us?

5. Read James 1:5-8. What principles does this text teach about understanding God's will?

Since God promises to give us wisdom, do you believe that God has given you all the tools you need to make wise decisions, even when you are uncertain about which path to choose? Why or why not?

6. If God gives us freedom to make choices as long as we remain within God's grand design, why do we still need to ask God for guidance?

THREE

The Role
of the Holy Spirit
in Guidance

◆

AFTER graduating from college in Portland, I traveled to Chicago to attend Trinity Evangelical Divinity School. The director of Chicago North Shore Young Life, a Christian ministry to high-school students, offered me a part-time staff position to lead the Deerfield Young Life Club.

The local Young Life committee put together a party a week before school began so that I could meet the club kids. I didn't know what to expect as I drove to the get-together. All I remember is my disappointment that there were only twenty kids in attendance—eighteen girls and two guys! The kids were enthusiastic about starting the club, but I thought, *There's no way I can start a club with only two guys!* That night I wrote in my prayer journal, "I will not start until I meet and know the names of fifty young men in the school."

The first week of school I set out for the high school during lunch hour to meet some kids. I had spent a lot of time with teenagers during my college days, but no amount of experience could take away the terror of walking into a school of twenty-six hundred kids where I knew practically no one. At the party a week earlier, I had met a junior named Mike O'Shea. So before I entered the school, I prayed that God would help me find him. I was certain he liked me and felt he would be my ticket to meeting other guys. But what were the odds of running into one out of twenty-six hundred kids? I was asking God to perform a mathematical miracle, but it was the only way I could think of to meet guys and get the ministry going.

As I whispered my prayer, I put my hand on the cold steel handle of the double doors leading into the school. The doors opened to a huge common area with two large hallways funneling into it. I found this common area strangely empty except for one guy just entering the far end from one of the hallways. I couldn't believe my eyes. It was none other than Mike O'Shea, and he was happy to see me. He was just heading to the lunchroom, where he introduced me to two dozen or more guys and sat me down in the middle of them. That answered prayer assured me that God wanted me in this ministry and that the Holy Spirit was going to be with me every step of the way.

The Holy Spirit dwells within every believer. Jesus told his disciples that the Holy Spirit "will guide you into all truth" (Jn 16:13). The Holy Spirit inspires us to know when to pray and what to pray, and communicates with us when we listen. A life of prayer and communion with the Holy Spirit is at the heart of New Testament teaching about guidance.

The Holy Spirit may not lead us to find the one and only right path to take in each situation, but he leads us to make wise choices. He does this in ten ways: through prayer, listening, Scripture, dreams and visions, goals and information, counsel, hindsight, feelings, circumstances and conscience.

Prayer

The Spirit guides us by teaching us to pray about all our concerns. Paul tells us to worry about nothing but to pray about everything (Phil 4:6). God wants us to talk to him about every decision we make. We should not pray for God to show us the only choice in his will but to help us make wise choices.

One of the best places to look in Scripture for guidance by means of prayer is the Psalms. Their help lies not in offering specific advice but in showing us how to maintain a love relationship with God. They are journals of authors who were brutally honest with their God. Read through a few psalms in one sitting and you will see the writers rail at God for his seeming absence, honor him for his power, doubt him because of his apparent forgetfulness of his promises, praise him for his mercy, question him for his failure to guide clearly and thank him for his deliverance. Regardless of what happens, God is never far from their thoughts. They practice the presence of God in daily details and talk freely to God about everything. In talking to him about the details in our lives, we learn what God is leading us to do.

When I was in my last two years at Lewis and Clark College in Portland, Oregon, the senior pastor of a Presbyterian church asked me to oversee his church's junior-high, senior-high and college programs during the summer. As I reported for work the second summer, the pastor told me of a young woman he had recruited to be on my staff team. When she reported to the first leaders' meeting, I found that I was attracted to her. Before long we began to see each other socially. By the end of the summer we had gotten serious.

She returned to college, and I set out for Trinity Evangelical Divinity School in Illinois. For the next four months our relationship was confined to letter writing and late-night phone calls. We agreed I would fly out to visit her before Christmas.

She met me at Portland International Airport, and we enjoyed three wonderful days together. On our last night, we exchanged Christmas presents. Then she announced, "I think we should put the brakes on our relationship." I couldn't believe my ears.

In January I returned to Trinity a discouraged man. I felt terribly alone. Although I continued to write letters to her, none of them were answered. I learned that "put the brakes on" meant "bring the relationship to a full stop." I went through my studies in a daze.

Then one day I prayed, "Lord, I'm really disappointed that Julie broke up with me. If it be your will, I would like to get back together with her. But I know you give only good gifts. You say, 'If you, then, though you are evil, know how to give good gifts to your children, how much more will your Father in heaven give good gifts to those who ask him!' [Mt 7:11]. If you choose not to grant my request, it can only mean that you have someone better for me. So I am going to quit feeling sorry for myself and trust you."

I am certain God had just been waiting for me to offer a prayer like that. All he needed to hear was that I trusted him completely. When I rose from my knees, I felt like a new man. The depression that had hung over me like early-morning fog suddenly lifted. I felt a renewed confidence that the Lord was answering my prayers and would do what was best for me. The young woman and I never did get back together, but God helped me handle the loss.

Three months later God introduced me to Jorie. She was recently widowed—her husband had died of cancer two years into their marriage. The head Young Life staff woman of the Chicago North Shore suggested that Jorie become coleader of the Deerfield Young Life Club. She was beautiful. She was also mature in Christ. The two-year period of fighting for her husband's life and working through his eventual death had caused her to grow deeply in her faith. God knit us together in love. A year and a half later we were married.

This experience taught me something important about prayer and God's will. As I honestly poured out my feelings to God in prayer, I came to trust that God was looking out for me and would give what was best for me. As I shared my thoughts with God day after day, I gradually began to understand his will for me. He showed me that it was okay to be sad about losing a meaningful relationship but that he was using that experience to prepare me for somebody who was better suited for me.

Jorie has character qualities and strengths that have been essential in helping me to become more conformed to Christ. Her experience, creativity, wisdom and perseverance have been invaluable to our work together. God knew who I needed better than I did. All he needed was for me to trust him.

The Holy Spirit also guides us through answered prayer. The Spirit led many biblical saints by answering specific prayers. Abraham did not want his son, Isaac, to marry a Canaanite woman, so he sent his servant to find a wife for Isaac from among Abraham's people. When the servant arrived, he prayed that God would show him success by granting that the girl he asked to draw drinking water for him would show herself to be the girl God had chosen for Isaac by offering to water his camels as well. Before he had finished praying, Rebekah, one of Abraham's relatives, came out with her jar on her shoulder. She was beautiful. The servant asked her for a drink. She gave him water to drink and offered to water the camels as well. God answered his prayer and assured him that he had come to the right place to find a wife for Isaac (Gen 24:12-67).

The Holy Spirit still guides us through answered prayer. Virginia Whitman shares a remarkable account of the Spirit's guidance. A woman from the village of La Mancha was visiting her invalid brother in Madrid. During her stay, she wanted to attend an evangelical church. Unable to locate one or find anyone to direct her, she asked the Holy Spirit for guidance. It occurred to her while praying to take a bus to the city center and wait upon God to do the rest. Her brother felt that his sister was crazy to look for a small church in a city of millions, especially since she was blind. But neither her blindness nor the magnitude of the obstacle before her hindered her faith. With great expectations, she boarded a bus, trusting God to lead her.

At the next stop, another woman got on and occupied the seat beside the visiting Christian. Sensing someone beside her, the blind Christian reached into her purse and fumbled for a gospel booklet. With a gentle witness for Jesus, the blind woman handed the message to the woman beside her. As they conversed, it became apparent that the Madrid resident was on her way to church. The blind woman quickly asked, "Could you possibly tell me where the First Baptist Church is?" To her utter amazement, the other woman answered, "Why, that's exactly where I'm going. You can go with me."[1]

I also find that the Holy Spirit guides me into God's will by prompting me to pray. Numerous times I have felt an urgency to pray for someone. Later I learned that person was going through a particular travail at that moment.

Recently my wife traveled to Russia to bring home four children processed for adoption by Orphans Overseas. Their adoptive American families anxiously awaited their arrival. Jorie and I made a point to talk to each other by phone every two days so that she could keep me apprised of prayer requests. We find that international adoptions always require a lot of prayer. I would then notify the Orphans Overseas staff to pray for specific needs in the adoption process. There were some occasions, however, when staff members felt prompted to pray even when Jorie had not instructed us to do so. Later we learned that these urgings to pray occurred at moments when Jorie was in special need. There were times when Jorie needed prayer support but was not able to contact us. During these times, she simply asked the Holy Spirit to notify us of our need to pray, and we were led to pray in answer to her prayer.

I find it comforting to know that when I am in need and separated from all Christian contact, I can ask the Holy Spirit to call people to pray. The Spirit can lead people into the knowledge that it is God's will at that moment for them to uphold a brother or sister in prayer.

Listening

Another way we experience guidance from the Holy Spirit is listening. When you pray, do you take time to listen to God? Prayer is not a one-way street. It involves talking to God, of course, but we should also give God an opportunity to talk with us.

We are told that the reason the *Titanic* hit and was sunk by an iceberg was that the ship's radios were completely jammed for several hours with ship-to-shore conversations between passengers and friends or family in Britain and America. Other ships in the area were not able to get through with a warning signal. This serves as a warning to us. God says, "Don't jam the communication lines of prayer with so much talk about what you want that I can't get through to you."

To hear from God, we have to be quiet. God speaks through a still, small voice. Often during personal Bible study and prayer, I ask, "God, is there something you want to say to me?" Then I listen. Sometimes I take a piece of paper and put at the top "Dear Ron" and at the bottom "Love, God." Then I write what I think he wants me to hear. Or I imagine myself standing before Christ on Judgment Day talking about the decision I am about to make. It helps me choose the course of action I would feel best about reporting to Christ.

Sometimes I hear from the Holy Spirit in the form of an inward impression or strong conviction. Most people testify that when they became Christians they felt an internal nudge that drove them into the arms of Christ. Jesus said, "No one can come to me unless the Father who sent me draws him" (Jn 6:44). Who draws us to Christ? God, in the person of the Holy Spirit. The wonderful news is that the Holy Spirit doesn't leave us as baby Christians. He continues to tug at us to learn more and to become more like Christ. If we are to listen to his voice, we must tune our antennas to the frequency of the Holy Spirit.

How do we hear the Holy Spirit's still, small voice? We have to get away from televisions, radios, telephones, fax machines and all the hurry and noise that crowds our lives and get quiet before God. We need to listen to the Holy Spirit, and seldom does listening come in five-minute spurts. If we want to sense the Spirit's leading, we do well to set aside large blocks of time. Possibly an hour early in the morning, or a two-to-three-hour block of time, or a whole day, or even a several-day retreat. Read God's Word, meditate on its truths, take time to pray, but don't forget to set aside time to listen to God. God declares in Psalm 46:10, "Be still and know that I am God." The Holy Spirit is most apt to speak when we take time to be still.

Jesus developed the discipline of stillness before God. In spite of his pressing schedule, "very early in the morning, while it was still dark, Jesus got up, left the house and went off to a solitary place, where he prayed" (Mk 1:35). Be honest. When do you make time for stillness and solitude? What do you do to still your racing mind and body so that you can hear the Spirit speak to you?

As I learn to listen to the Spirit in times of quiet, I begin to pick up his frequency throughout the day. When I am counseling, he may give me insight to the root problem a person may be facing. I may sense a leading to probe a certain area. Sometimes the Spirit reminds me that I need to ask forgiveness of someone or that I need to encourage a friend. At times I feel an urge to call a person. Listening is a difficult discipline. I'm not naturally quiet. But it is essential if I am to hear his inner leadings.

A church member shared with me about a friend who was traveling in Uganda in the early seventies during the ruthless rule of Idi Amin. Thousands of Ugandans who disagreed with his policies were put to death. As this man and his family were driving one day, he felt a sudden urge from the Spirit to stop, get out of the car and flee into the bush. Stopping the car along the side of the road, they took a few of their belongings, slipped into the bush and continued by foot. Later they learned that just around the bend Amin had set up a roadblock, and his soldiers were murdering people who were in opposition to the government.

On the afternoon of June 14, 1955, Thomas Whittaker, a welder from Boston, got a sudden and strong hunch that something was wrong. He didn't know what it was, but he sensed it so strongly that he quit work and got into his car and started driving. At various stoplights, he tried to turn his car toward home, but the intuition kept driving him. Time after time he turned toward Washington Street, where his company was doing some work.

This is ridiculous, he kept telling himself. *That Washington Street job has been suspended.* But he kept edging toward the area just the same. When he got there, he looked down into a fourteen-foot-deep trench that had been dug down the center of the street, and there in the bottom he saw a cave-in. The sides of the trench had collapsed. And projecting out of the tons of dirt, sand and debris was a human hand.

Whittaker jumped down into the trench and tried to claw away the dirt with his own hands. He dug down deep enough to uncover a wrist watch, and immediately he recognized it as belonging to his best friend and boss, John H. Sullivan, owner of the welding service. The hand moved. Frantic now, Whittaker scrambled to the top of the trench and called for the fire company and police to help dig Sullivan out of the hole.

Hours later, safe if not entirely sound, after his ordeal of being buried alive, Sullivan said he had decided to finish some work when the sides of the trench had suddenly given way. The only thing that saved him from immediate suffocation was that he was wearing his welder's mask. Inside of it, enough air was trapped to keep him alive until help came. Had he called for help? Indeed he had. At first he yelled out loud, and then, when it became clear that it would do no good, he began sending out mental distress signals like an SOS. "God send someone," he prayed. "God send someone." While he was praying, Whittaker had begun to get his sudden urge to visit the Washington Street scene.[2]

Remember, when you pray, the Holy Spirit can dispatch an answer in seconds. But if you are to be his messenger, you must be responsive to his voice. The Holy Spirit guides you, but you have to be sensitive to his leading. If you stopped and listened to the Spirit right now, what do you think he might say to you? Might he be saying "It's time you gave your life to Christ"? If the joy of knowing Christ is gone, might he be saying "You've lost your first love. Things aren't the way they used to be. Return to Christ"? If you're worried about something, could the message be "Trust me"? If you're faced with a major decision, might he say "I'll give you the wisdom to make a good decision"?

Scripture

Another way the Spirit leads us is through Scripture. The Bible reveals God's grand design for all Christians. The Holy Spirit gives us a desire to read Holy Writ and then helps us to understand it. Jesus said, "When he, the Spirit of truth, comes, he will guide you into all truth. He will not speak on his own; he will speak only what he hears, and he will tell you what is yet to come. He will bring glory to me by taking from what is mine and making it known to you" (Jn 16:13-14).

The Holy Spirit also helps us identify if a given decision will cause us to violate God's grand design. In any decision we are contemplating, one of the first questions to ask is this: Are there any commands of Scripture that relate to this decision? The Holy Spirit will bring scriptures to mind and help us see what light God's Word sheds on our decision.

Although I do not recommend flipping open your Bible and asking for a verse to guide you as the best way to use the Bible, there have been times I've asked God to show me something in his Word to shed light on a choice before me. He has directed me to passages that cause me to reflect on the impact a given decision will have on my faith, family or church.

Scripture is of the greatest help when we understand its purpose. It gives general principles for how God wants us to live. It tells us if a given choice might cause us to stray from God's grand design. The best way to use Scripture is to read it faithfully and to know it so well that it permeates every decision. As you become more familiar with the whole counsel of God and obey its instructions, God will give you wisdom in all your decisions.

Dreams and Visions

The Holy Spirit also guides us through dreams and visions. Angels appeared to many people in the New Testament through dreams or visions: Zechariah (Lk 1:11), Mary (Lk 1:26), Joseph on two different occasions (Mt 1:20; 2:13), Saul (Act 9:3), Ananias (Acts 9:11-16), Cornelius (Acts 10:3), Peter (Acts 10:9), Paul (Acts 16:9-13; 18:9-10; 27:22-26). Add to these all the people led by dreams or visions in the Old Testament, and we see that this has been a common form of guidance.

There is no reason to believe that the Spirit does not continue to lead Christians through dreams and visions today. Jorie dreamed one night of a woman she had discipled as a high-school and college-age student being in trouble. The next morning she said, "I think I need to call her." When she called, she learned that this young woman was dating a nonbeliever and was out of fellowship with God. As a result of Jorie's meeting with her, she got back on track with the Lord, started coming to our church and became active again in Christian service.

Victor Landero, a humble farmer in the tiny village of Corozalito, Colombia, South America, had a strong desire to evangelize. One night he dreamed about a house in the forest. It was an ordinary house, but he had never seen that particular one before. He heard a voice saying, "The people in that house are dying without Christ, because no one ever told them of him." Victor heard the voice several more times, but he dismissed the dream from his mind.

Eight months later, Victor told the Lord he would tell those people of Christ if God showed him where to go. He took a companion and went to look for the house. At noon on the second day, he found the house in a clearing in the woods, just as he had seen it in his dream.

The woman who came out as he approached was astounded when

she heard Victor's request for a meeting that night in her house. She had already seen him in a dream, three days earlier, standing in her home, which was crowded with people. That night, all twenty-four of the neighbors came and received Christ. The next night, they all returned with ten more people. At the end of that night, there were thirty-four new believers in Christ.[3]

I am not suggesting that dreams and visions become our primary source of inspiration. We have God's Word, which contains all the information we need for holy living. But we must not limit God. If the Holy Spirit chooses to communicate with you through a dream or vision, be ready to listen. But remember, nothing you receive through extrabiblical means can disagree with Scripture. Test the content of your dreams or visions against the Bible.

Goals and Information

Another way the Spirit guides is through the use of goals and information. If you want to make wise decisions, gather information about your gifts, interests, passions and goals. When you give your life to Christ, you are given spiritual gifts. Find out what your gifts are. Some people struggle to ascertain God's will for their lives, not realizing that His will is written into their very beings. We find it in our spiritual gifts, passions and interests.[4]

I spend six hours in our membership class teaching about spiritual gifts. Many people tell me that not only did the teaching unlock for them ways God wanted to use them in ministry, but the discovery of their gifts was also instrumental in helping them find the right vocation. Of course—what else would we expect? You and I are going to use the spiritual gifts God has given us the rest of our lives in ministry, in work and in whatever we do.

You determine your life goals by taking stock of your own spiritual gifts, special abilities and passions and then by writing out your life goals. Ask yourself, *When I reach the end of my life, what do I want to have accomplished? For what do I want to be known?* Then ask yourself, *If I am to fulfill my life goals, what goals do I need to pursue this year?* Your lifelong ambitions will help you decide what choices you need to be making today. In prayer, ask God what goals he wants you to pursue this year.

In addition to knowing our goals, we need to gather all the relevant facts necessary to make an informed decision. I find it helpful to write out the pros and cons of the possibilities before me. Often I find a number of issues of which I am uncertain. The uncertainty tells me I need to gather more information.

When I graduated from seminary, I candidated at six churches. I didn't know which church to choose. So Jorie and I listed the pros and cons of each ministry and compared their merits. Wherever we had uncertainties, we made notes of questions we still had to ask. Once we made this list and felt that we had good answers to our questions, the wisest choice soon became apparent to us. As we gathered information and prayed about the data we compiled, the Spirit was better able to lead us.

Counsel

Still another way the Holy Spirit guides us is through the provision of wise counsel. Before making major decisions, seek the advice of people you consider wise and discerning. When King Hezekiah was threatened by the king of Assyria, he sought the counsel of the prophet Isaiah (2 Kings 19:2). Before Jehoshaphat went into battle against Ramath Gilead he insisted on seeking the advice of a prophet (2 Chron 18:4).

The book of Proverbs suggests that you approach many advisers:
For lack of guidance a nation falls,
    but many advisers make victory sure. (Prov 11:14)
Plans fail for lack of counsel,
    but with many advisers they succeed. (Prov 15:22)
Don't just go to people you know will support the decision you favor, but seek the counsel of a broad range of people.

Without a doubt, my finest adviser is my wife, Jorie. I try to never move forward with a decision unless she and I are in agreement. One reason God instituted the ordinance of marriage was to help two people living together to make better choices. Before making important decisions, I seek the counsel of my wife, my children, trusted friends, elders, fellow staff or mentors in the faith. I don't always like what they say, and sometimes wish I hadn't asked, but I know I make better choices as a result of their input.

One way to receive good counsel is to imagine yourself counseling someone you have never met before about the identical decision you are contemplating. Determine what you would tell this person, and then take the advice that you would readily give to another for whom you want the best.

Hindsight

Another important way the Holy Spirit guides is through the process of looking back at how God has led in the past. For me, guidance is most evident when I look back. In the midst of a decision, the best choice is seldom crystal clear. If I saw what God wanted me to do in advance—a paint-by-numbers scheme—that would leave no room for faith. I have to step out in faith. But through hindsight, I see how God led me. By looking back at how God led me in the past, I learn how he may be leading me today.

When Jorie and I were deciding about my becoming pastor of Sunset Presbyterian Church, not all the counsel we received was positive. Nevertheless, we felt a quiet confidence that it was the right decision to make. The congregation at the time was deeply wounded. Very few members showed up for Sunday worship. The elders had discussed closing the doors and shutting down the church. The presbytery executive counseled against my taking the position. It had been a church torn by strife for years. Other people I counseled with who knew the church recommended that I pass on the opportunity.

Yet, as I looked back at ways God had led me in the past and at what God had been doing in my life, I could see ways that God had been preparing me for Sunset. I recognized feelings of restlessness I had in my former ministry and an eagerness to take on a church that was struggling. I realized that principles I had learned in a growing youth ministry had prepared me for shepherding a church that was in desperate need of new life.

So in spite of the counsel I received to the contrary, I accepted the call. Today, fourteen years later, we see all kinds of reasons God wanted us to come to Sunset. In hindsight we see that Sunset has been the perfect place for me to minister. Clare and Savilla Hoskins, two charter members who lived through all the difficult times the church has known, told me, "We believe you were made for Sunset. Sunset has been waiting for you all these years." The church has grown steadily the past fourteen years. When I first came we rejoiced to have one hundred people in worship. Today we have fourteen hundred people in worship each Sunday. When I first came, there were days when I was the only person in the building. Today we have programs sixteen to eighteen hours a day, seven days a week. Hundreds of people have come to Christ through the ministries of Sunset. By looking back at ways God has led me in the past, I can better discern ways God may be leading me today.

Feelings

Another important way the Spirit leads us is through our feelings. Learn to pay attention to your gut-level feelings and convictions. I believe in sanctified feelings. If we are filled with the Holy Spirit, he impresses upon us what would be a wise choice. The longer I live, the more I come to trust my gut-level instincts about what is best. When I have considered a matter from every conceivable viewpoint, if my mind tells me one thing and my heart tells me something else, I follow my heart.

When Jorie and I were making our decision about coming to Sunset Presbyterian, we scheduled a three-day trip to give us time to pray about and discuss our decision. After praying extensively and discussing at length the opportunity before us, we returned with a gut-level feeling that God was leading us to go to Sunset and that he was going to do a great work through us. We came home with a quiet assurance.

Circumstances

We saw in chapter one that a preoccupation with circumstances can lead to immaturity in decision-making. For example, if you think God has only one person for you to date, and you are looking for circumstantial evidence to help you select a date, it can lead to strange dating methodologies—like the collegian who was looking for God's will in his telephone calls. If the phone was busy when he called a young woman, that meant she was not the one. If there was no answer, he was to call again. If she said no, God didn't want him to date her (not to mention that the girl didn't want him to date her either). If she said yes, she was the one.

I heard of one young lady, a flight attendant, who had just returned from a vacation in the Rockies. During this magical week of mountain peaks, blue skies and sweet-smelling pines, she fell in love with a very eligible bachelor. He owned and operated a cattle ranch and lived in a log cabin. At the end of the week, Mr. Wonderful proposed. This young lady had never been good at making up her mind, but she returned home to her job feeling that she would somehow be guided. The next day, while in flight, she found herself wondering what to do. To perk up, she stopped in the restroom and splashed a bit of cool water on her face. There was some turbulence, and a sign lit up: PLEASE RETURN TO THE CABIN. That was her guidance. So she returned to the cabin in the mountains.

Although looking for God's will in circumstances can be abused, that does not mean that the Holy Spirit cannot guide us through circumstances. Gideon prayed for a sign so that he would know God's will. God called him to lead the Israelites against the Midianites. Since the Midianite army vastly outnumbered them, Gideon wanted to make sure he wasn't making a mistake. He asked that there be dew on a wool fleece but that the surrounding ground be dry. After God accomplished this miraculous sign, Gideon asked God to reverse the process. Once again, God did so (Judg 6:36-40).

Sometimes the Holy Spirit leads us by closing doors or answering no to our prayers. The apostle Paul prayed to minister in the Roman province of Asia, but we read that he was kept by the Holy Spirit from preaching the Word there (Acts 16:6-10). How did the Spirit block Paul from entering that province? Presumably by closing doors or failing to open doors for him to gain passage into the region. Possibly the flights were full, they lost their visas, or the Judean embassy didn't process their passports.

God still uses circumstances to guide his people. An illness, a healing, a war, a famine, a heavy crop, drought, rain—all are signs. Jesus himself rebukes his detractors for being able to discern meteorological signs while not perceiving the signs of God. We must learn to interpret the phenomena in our lives to determine if God is speaking to us through them. Could it be that it was God who brought us up short by means of a painful failure, which at first we did not understand—a serious illness or a strange hesitation? Was it he who guided us by means of a success, and so opened up a new and unexpected horizon?

I think the way to avoid misusing circumstantial signs is to make them some of the last signs you follow for guidance. If you have prayed, listened to God, searched the Scriptures, determined your goals, gathered information, sought counsel, examined your feelings, and still feel a need for more guidance, then you can pray, "God, I feel this is the best course of action. If you disagree, please shut the doors so I know there is a better decision for me to make."

Even Francis Schaeffer resorted to fleece laying in a moment of crisis, when he felt a deep need to know God's will. It was 5:30 a.m. on the day that nineteen-year-old Fran was to leave for college to prepare for the ministry. At his father's request Fran got up early to see him before he went to work. When Fran came downstairs, his dad said, "I don't want a son who is a minister, and I don't want you to go." Since Fran had first started talking about being a preacher, his relations with his parents had been strained. For six years his education had been geared toward mechanical engineering. His dad wanted a son who would be "a good honest worker, not a parasite."

Fran broke the awkward silence and asked permission to go to the cellar to pray. There he tearfully begged God to make clear what to do. In desperation he took out a coin and said, "Heads, I'll go in spite of Dad." He flipped the coin, and it came up heads. Still crying, he pleaded, "God, be patient with me. If it comes up tails this time, I'll go." The tossed coin was tails. A third time he begged more earnestly. "Once more, God, I don't want to make a mistake with Dad upstairs. Please, now let it be heads again." After the coin came up heads, a reassured Fran mounted the cellar stairs and confidently told his dad that he had to go. The young Francis Schaeffer had faced a crucial decision that went against his parents' wishes and dreams. Reminiscent of Gideon's fleece, a thrice-flipped coin brought certainty at a time of family opposition. Viewed from the perspective of Schaeffer's productive life and ministry, those flips of a coin seem even more significant than they did that morning.[5]

We must be careful in reading circumstantial signs, however. Some people who are facing intense opposition in ministry draw the conclusion that they must be out of the will of God or they wouldn't be having so many problems. But you could just as well read the troubles as an indication that you are in God's will, for the Bible tells us that we will face opposition.

Conscience

One more important way the Holy Spirit leads us is through our conscience. Jesus tells us that the Spirit convicts us of sin (Jn 16:8). When the Holy Spirit enters our lives, he cultivates a sensitive conscience. This enlightened conscience becomes one of God's finest means of leading his people.

The writer to the Hebrews describes how the Holy Spirit transforms our conscience:

> This is the covenant I will make with the house of Israel after that time, declares the Lord. I will put my laws in their minds and write them on their hearts. (Heb 8:10; compare Jer 31:33)
>
> How much more, then, will the blood of Christ, who through the eternal Spirit offered himself unblemished to God, cleanse our consciences from acts that lead to death, so that we may serve the living God! (Heb 9:14)
>
> Let us draw near to God with a sincere heart in full assurance of faith, having our hearts sprinkled to cleanse us from a guilty conscience. (Heb 10:22)

Paul tells Timothy that "the goal of this command is love, which comes from a pure heart and a good conscience and a sincere faith" (1 Tim 1:5). The Spirit seeks to develop a conscience that is responsive to his promptings. When we have a healthy conscience that is in tune with the Spirit, we grow strong in our faith. But when we fail to cultivate a sensitive conscience, we put ourselves in a perilous position (1 Tim 1:19).

The Holy Spirit leads us by fostering a conscience sensitive to right and wrong. When we are living in obedience to Christ and making decisions that are wise, we can expect a sense of peace: "Let the peace of Christ rule in your hearts, since as members of one body you were called to peace" (Col 3:15). The peace of Christ is an inner calm and quiet assurance that comes from making good choices. After I have made an important decision, I like to sit on it for several days without telling anyone about my decision. If I feel good about the decision, it is probably a good one. If I lack peace, I often review the decision.

The Last Word

Late one evening a professor sat at his desk working on the next day's lectures. He shuffled through the papers and mail placed there by his housekeeper. As he threw them in the wastebasket, one magazine— not even addressed to him but delivered to his office by mistake— caught his attention. It fell open to an article entitled "The Needs of the Congo Mission."

The professor began reading it idly, but then he was consumed by these words: "The need is great here. We have no one to work in the northern province of Gabon in the central Congo. And it is my prayer as I write this article that God will lay his hand on one—one on whom, already, the Master's eyes have been cast—that he or she shall be called to this place to help us."

The professor closed the magazine and wrote in his diary: "My search is over." He gave himself to go to the Congo. The professor's name was Albert Schweitzer. That little article, hidden in a periodical intended for someone else, was placed by accident in Schweitzer's mailbox. By chance his housekeeper put the magazine on the professor's desk. By chance he noticed the title, which seemed to leap out at him. Dr. Schweitzer became a great figure in a humanitarian work nearly unmatched in human history. Was that all by chance? No. It was God's guidance.[6]

The Holy Spirit will show you what Christ wants you to do. But you've got to stay alert . . . listen for his voice . . . and be obedient. The Spirit does not guide you to find the one and only choice that is in his will. There are numerous options you can choose and still be in God's will. He gives you freedom to make choices as long as you stay within the parameters of his grand design. His guidance helps you make wise choices within the freedom he gives you.

He will suit the message to your need, but the central truth is certain: We serve a God who has led in history, who still leads today and who wants to lead us. But we've got to stay tuned. Are you on the Spirit's frequency?

Questions for Reflection and Discussion

1. Of the ten ways the Holy Spirit guides us, which have been most meaningful to you in your own decision-making?

2. How has the Holy Spirit led you through answered prayer or prompting you to pray?

3. What are some ways you feel the Holy Spirit has led you through a dream or vision?

4. If circumstances are one of the ways the Spirit leads us, what is the difference between using circumstances in a way that leads to wise decision-making and using them in an immature way?

5. What principle or insight was most helpful to you in this chapter?

FOUR

Why Prayer Is Essential to Discovering God's Will

◆

I HAD been in Romania for one week attempting to adopt a baby girl. Two months earlier my wife, Jorie, had identified a newborn in an orphanage in Bucharest. In overseas adoptions, both prospective parents have to see the child in its country if they want to finalize the adoption overseas. Otherwise they must go through proceedings in the United States before the adoption is finalized. So I had flown to Romania to see our prospective daughter, complete the adoption and bring her home.

The court hearing was set in Bucharest, so I flew the baby's seventeen-year-old birth mom there for our court appearance. She asked if she could go to the orphanage with me to see baby Andrea. I consented. That was a mistake. The mother spent most of the day with me as I took Andrea for a physical and had her tested for the HIV virus and hepatitis B. As we traveled to the hospital and to the doctor, I let the birth mom hold cuddly little Andrea. I watched her fall in love with the adorable baby she had never cuddled, except when she gave birth to her weeks earlier. By the day's end, I feared that the wonderful time with the baby might cause her to change her mind and back out of the adoption.

The next morning my worst fears were confirmed. The birth mom had run away, apparently deciding against going through with the adoption. We missed our court date.

With heavy heart I picked up the phone to call Jorie with the heartbreaking news. But to my surprise, Jorie did not appear shaken. She assured me that she and our boys would pray that the mother would be found and that she would agree that it was in her best interest and the baby's to go ahead with the adoption.

Jorie, twelve-year-old Tad, ten-year-old David and seven-year-old Luke fasted and prayed for an entire day. Tad told me later, "I nearly died, but I did it for you and Drea." With their prayer support, things began to change in Romania. The depression that had hung over me like a dark cloud lifted. I felt a renewed sense of hope. I felt like Martin Luther must have when he said, "I feel like someone is praying for me."

Three days later we located the birth mom at her home in northern Romania. To our relief, she once again agreed that it was best to go through with the adoption. A new court date was set, the papers were signed, and I flew home with Drea.

What made the difference? Prayer. People prayed for me and Andrea, and God moved on our behalf. God works when we pray.

Jesus Prayed

Since God works when we pray, clearly it is God's will that we pray. With all the power available to us through prayer, isn't it strange that we find it difficult to find time to pray?

Our Lord took time to pray. The disciples testify to that. They heard Jesus get up early, long before dawn, to pray (Mk 1:35). They saw that after healing a leper and many sick people, he went away by himself to pray (Lk 5:16). They knew that he prayed through the night prior to choosing them (Lk 6:12).

After one of Jesus' seasons of prayer, his disciples asked him to teach them to pray. You can almost hear them: "Lord, when we pray we can't think what to say after a few minutes, but you pray through the night. We yawn and grow sleepy when we pray, but you stay alert for hours. What's your secret?"

Jesus responded by teaching them what we call "the Lord's Prayer." Then he added,

So I say to you: Ask and it will be given to you; seek and you will find; knock and the door will be opened to you. For everyone who asks receives; he who seeks finds; and to him who knocks, the door will be opened.

Which of you fathers, if your son asks for a fish, will give him a snake instead? Or if he asks for an egg, will give him a scorpion? If you then, though you are evil, know how to give good gifts to your children, how much more will your Father in heaven give the Holy Spirit to those who ask him! (Lk 11:9-13)

Jesus is teaching us that, just as fathers love to give to their kids, God loves to give to us. It is God's will for you to pray. So pray.

Tremendous power is available in prayer, God loves to give to us when we ask and it is God's will that we pray. So why is it so difficult for us to pray? How is it that we seldom find time to pray? The average person spends more time each week talking to answering machines than to the Lord. It is estimated that the average church member in America prays less than twenty minutes a week. Statistics show that the average pastor spends only ten minutes a day in prayer. Most Christians view prayer as the thing to do when all else fails. *Prayer is fine,* we think, *but the real action is elsewhere.* We find it difficult to pray for at least five reasons.

Why We Find It Difficult to Pray

Spiritual forces of evil frustrate our attempts at prayer. The apostle Paul tells us that "our struggle is not against flesh and blood, but against . . . spiritual forces of evil" (Eph 6:12). Satan knows the power of prayer and does everything in his power to keep us from praying. So don't be amazed at the distractions and interruptions that crowd into your life when you set aside time to pray. They do not come by coincidence. They are carefully orchestrated attempts by the enemy to keep you from prayer. John writes, "The whole world is under the control of the evil one" (1 Jn 5:19), and again Paul writes, "The god of this age has blinded the minds of unbelievers, so that they cannot see the light of the gospel of the glory of Christ" (2 Cor 4:4). If Satan controls the whole world and blinds unbelievers from the truth of Christ, you can be sure he tries to keep Christians from wielding the mighty power of prayer.

Jesus tells us, "When a strong man, fully armed, guards his own house, his possessions are safe. But when someone stronger attacks and overpowers him, he takes away the armor in which the man trusted and divides up the spoils" (Lk 11:21-22). When we pray, God overpowers the spiritual forces of evil that hold people in bondage. When we fail to pray, our spiritual enemies don't worry about our efforts. They know that without prayer all our other efforts are doomed to failure. But, when we pray, we invade enemy territory and establish the kingdom of God.

We do not recognize that God is our only hope. We embrace the misguided notion that we can handle most problems and need God only in emergencies. We try everyone and everything else before admitting that God is our only hope. But James said, "You do not have, because you do not ask God" (Jas 4:2).

There are people who, in their journey, have come to us. They work in the same office with us, sit behind us at school, live next door—and we are the only Christians they meet. Our meager resources should make us desperate. We feel like the host: "I have nothing to set before him" (Lk 11:6). His words echo our own desperation in the face of the responsibilities God has given us.

"Lord, my neighbor's teenage son died in an auto accident—and I have nothing to set before her."

"Lord, my friend is lost and dying of AIDS—and I have nothing to set before him."

"Lord, the woman I work with . . . her home is breaking up—and I have nothing to set before her."

None of us have the resources to meet these needs. That should drive us to God in prayer. It's God's will for us to pray so that we learn that our only hope is in him. Ron Dunn in his book *Don't Just Stand There, Pray Something* tells of an answer to prayer shared with him by a mother of a teenage son:

One day as she was getting a pie ready to put into the oven, the phone rang. It was the school nurse: Her son had come down with a high fever and would she come and take him home?

The mother calculated how long it would take to drive to school and back, and how long the pie should bake, and concluded there was enough time. Popping the pie in the oven, she left for school. When she arrived, her son's fever was worse and the nurse urged her to take him to the doctor. . . .

By the time she got the boy home and in bed and headed out again for the shopping mall, she was not only frayed, but frazzled and frantic as well. And she had forgotten about the pie in the oven. At the mall she found a pharmacy, got the prescription filled and rushed back to the car.

Which was locked.

Yes, there were her keys, hanging in the ignition switch, locked inside the car. She ran back into the mall, found a phone and called home. When her son finally answered, she blurted out, "I've locked the keys inside the car!"

The boy was barely able to speak. In a hoarse voice he whispered, "Get a wire coat hanger, Mom. You can get in with that." The phone went dead. . . . After combing through a dozen stores, she found one that was behind the times just enough to use wire hangers.

Hurrying out of the mall, she allowed herself a smile of relief. As she was about to step off the curb, she halted. She stared at the wire coat hanger.

"I don't know what to do with this!"

Then she remembered the pie in the oven. All the frustrations of the past hour collapsed on her and she began crying. Then she prayed, "Dear Lord, my boy is sick and he needs this medicine and my pie is in the oven and the keys are locked in the car and, Lord, I don't know what to do with this coat hanger. Dear Lord, send somebody who does know what to do with it, and I really need that person NOW, Lord. Amen."

She was wiping her eyes when a beat-up old car pulled up to the curb and stopped in front of her. A young man, twentyish-looking, in a T-shirt and ragged jeans, got out. The first thing she noticed about him was the long, stringy hair, and then the beard that hid everything south of his nose. He was coming her way. When he drew near she stepped in front of him and held out the wire coat hanger. "Young man," she said, "do you know how to get into a locked car with one of these?"

He gaped at her for a moment, then plucked the hanger from her hand. "Where's the car?"

She had never seen anything like it—it was simply amazing how easily he got into her car. A quick look at the door and window, a couple of twists of the coat hanger and bam! Just like that, the door was open.

When she saw the door open she threw her arms around him. "Oh," she said, "the Lord sent you! You're such a good boy. You must be a Christian."

He stepped back and said, "No ma'am, I'm not a Christian, and I'm not a good boy. I just got out of prison yesterday."

She jumped at him and she hugged him again—fiercely. "Bless God!" she cried. "He sent me a professional!"[1]

When she was in a fix, she prayed. She realized that only God could deliver her. It is God's will that we live with this same moment-by-moment dependence on him.

We do not understand how much God loves us. We tend to think that God is like the reluctant neighbor, quite unwilling to give us what we ask. We can't believe he really loves us and is ready to give us all that we need. This false notion of God demotivates us in our attempts to pray.

When the disciples asked Jesus to teach them to pray, he responded with the parable of the friend at midnight (Lk 11). He suggested to them that the thing that can motivate us to pray more than anything else is to understand that God loves us and longs to give us what we need. Martin Luther said, "Prayer is not overcoming God's reluctance, but laying hold of his willingness." Sometimes we fail to pray because we compare God with people we know who are like the reluctant neighbor. People aren't always there for us when we need them, but God is always available.

God always gives good gifts to us. Understanding that God loves me so much that he gives me only good gifts has strengthened my prayer life. I'm not afraid to ask God for anything, because I know he gives me only the things that are good for me.

He hears all your cries. He knows the anxiety you feel over an impending surgery or the exasperation you feel over a child's irresponsibility or the desperation you feel over the plight of your aging parents. These are matters of great magnitude to him because they are matters of great importance to you.

We do not fully appreciate the power in prayer. We will spend more time praying for others when we come to understand that there is much that is beyond our power to give people. If we truly love people, we will desire for them far more than is within our power to give them, and this will lead us to prayer. Praying is the most loving thing we can do for someone.

In God's work, nothing is more important than prayer. People today desperately need the help we can give them. Marriages are being shattered. Children are being destroyed. Individuals are living lives of quiet desperation, without purpose or a future. And we can make a difference . . . if we pray on their behalf.

Jim Vaus was a great hulk of a man. He was a preacher's kid, but he hated Christ. He was a brilliant man, so he tried to attain the best of both worlds. He worked for Mickey Cohen of the mafia in Los Angeles while at the same time working for the Los Angeles Police Department.

That was until 1949, when he went to a tent meeting where Billy Graham was preaching. At the end of the service they sang "Just As I Am," and Jim got ready to make a quick exit. Just as he turned to leave, a little guy about half his size pulled on his coat and said, "Wouldn't you like to know Jesus and go forward?" Vaus thought about hitting him in the chops and sending the little guy flying. But as he turned to wallop the little fellow, to his dismay he found that he was praying.

Vaus said later, "How can you hit a guy who's praying?" And

suddenly an incredible power came over him. As they sang the song he had heard many times as a boy, for the first time he understood it personally: "Just as I am without one plea, but that thy blood was shed for me." Jim went forward and gave his life to Christ. That's the power of prayer. No matter how determined Vaus was to keep Christ out of his life, God's love pursued him through prayer.

Do you know the power of prayer? How much do you pray for your friends, your mate, your children, your parents, your pastor, your president and elected leaders?

We give up far too quickly. Jesus said, "Everyone who asks receives" (Lk 11:10). "Asks" is in the present tense. It means to keep on asking. We need to continue to ask until we receive. George Müller, the founder of the New Orphan-Houses in Bristol, England, was known more than anything else for his commitment to prayer. He wrote,

> The great point is to never give up until the answer comes. I have been praying every day for 52 years for two men, sons of a friend of my youth. They are not converted yet, but they will be! The great fault of the children of God is that they do not continue in prayer— they do not go on praying; they do not persevere. If they desire anything for God's glory, they should pray until they get it.

One of these men became a Christian at George Müller's funeral, the other not until years later.[2]

Don't give up when you pray. It is God's will that you persevere in prayer. Don't be impatient. God invites you to bring all your needs to him in the knowledge that he loves to meet your heart's desires.

What Happens When God's People Pray?

We would pray more if we understood the amazing things that happen as a result of our prayer.

For one, governments are granted peace. Paul identifies some of the good results that occur when God's people pray: "I urge, then, first of all, that requests . . . be made . . . for kings and all those in authority, that we may live peaceful and quiet lives" (1 Tim 2:1-2). Christians are to pray for those in authority so that they may live in peace. When governments experience peace, the church is free to spread the news of Christ, for the gospel travels more easily in times of peace. Missionaries are kicked out of countries and people are not allowed to pass freely across borders in times of war.

If our prayers bring about peace, we still have a lot of praying to do. One needs only to look at a few of the places where the United Nations has recently stationed peacekeeping forces to realize that our world is at war: Bosnia, Somalia, Cambodia, El Salvador, Angola, Iraq and Mozambique, just to name a few. In the four years prior to my writing, the U.N. has launched fourteen peacekeeping operations, compared with just thirteen in the previous forty years.

Scripture teaches that the key to a great presidency is not so much the views and leadership capability of the president as the prayers of God's people. In 2 Chronicles 7:14 we read, "If my people, who are called by my name, will humble themselves and pray and seek my face and turn from their wicked ways, then will I hear from heaven and will forgive their sin and will heal their land." The health of our country lies not primarily with our president but with decisions you and I make: *if we turn from our sins and pray, God will heal our land.*

God is looking for Christians who will devote themselves to prayer. God says, "I looked for a man . . . who would build up the wall and stand before me in the gap on behalf of the land so I would not have to destroy it, but I found none" (Ezek 22:30). Are you one who stands in the gap and prays for our president and government leaders? Do you support your national and local leaders in prayer? Do you realize that your prayers can influence the course of national and local affairs?

There's a third positive result that occurs when we pray: *God's people live holy lives.* Paul's desire was "that we may live peaceful and quiet lives in all godliness and holiness. This is good, and pleases God our Savior" (1 Tim 2:2-3). For God's name to be honored, Christians must cultivate character traits of godliness. If we want God to receive honor and his name to be praised, we must pray for Christians everywhere. Just as we are to pray for government leaders, we are to pray for leaders in the church.

When Satan wants to destroy a church, he goes after the leaders. He tries to lead them into sin or discourage them. If you want a better pastor, don't run to another church; pray for the one you have. We have witnessed a marked decline in Christian morality in recent years.

Could one of the primary reasons for this demise be prayerlessness on the part of the church? Immorality among numerous Christian leaders has jolted the church. Maybe our failure to pray has, in part, led to the fall of these mighty warriors.

Samuel said, "Far be it from me that I should sin against the Lord by failing to pray for you" (1 Sam 12:23). If Samuel felt this way, I think that it is safe to say that we sin against the Lord when we do not pray for our Christian brothers and sisters. When we do pray, Christian leaders and friends are kept from falling to the temptations of the evil one.

Still a fourth good result that comes about when God's people pray is that *men and women find salvation:* God "wants all men to be saved and to come to a knowledge of the truth. For there is one God and one mediator between God and men, the man Christ Jesus" (1 Tim 2:4-5). Because God wants all people to know him, God wills that we pray, for when we do people come to salvation.

The Last Word

Paul wants to make certain that Timothy, his son in the faith, builds his ministry around prayer. He calls Timothy to lead the church at Ephesus in the discipline of prayer (1 Tim 2:1). The first mission of the church is to be a worshiping and praying community. Out of a healthy worship and prayer life, God enables us to minister to others. I am convinced that great things in God's kingdom happen when, and only when, God's people pray. Let me ask you, if you were convinced that prayer could bring about the salvation of your family members and friends, enable you to live a holy life, transform our leaders and bring peace to our world, would you be willing to increase your time in prayer? I commit myself to a deeper and greater prayer life. Will you?

If God has convicted you in this chapter, I invite you to bow your head right now and offer the following prayer.

Dear God, my lack of prayer for those in positions of authority stands as a testimony that I have not understood the tremendous power in prayer and my important role in shaping national and international affairs. Please forgive me. My lack of prayer for my friends and relatives and for people around the world who do not know you shows how little I know about the power of prayer. Forgive me. I covenant today to pray faithfully for our president and for local, national and international leaders. I also commit to praying faithfully for people you have placed in my life who do not know you.

Questions for Reflection and Discussion

1. Have you ever been in dire need, like I was in Romania, when you asked for prayer and then saw circumstances change dramatically?

2. What do you learn from Jesus' example of prayer?

3. Of the five reasons I list as to why people fail to pray, with which one do you most closely identify? Why?

4. How much do you pray for our president and government leaders?

What do you think would change if more Christians began to faithfully intercede for their leaders?

5. What principle or insight in this chapter was most helpful to you?

FIVE

Learning About Prayer from the Master

◆

A WELL-known business axiom counsels, "If you want to know something, ask an expert." If you want to know about hockey, talk to Wayne Gretzky. If you want to learn about basketball, ask Shaquille O'Neil. If you want advice on how to turn around a large corporation, speak with Lee Iacocca. If you're looking for tips in international diplomacy, call Henry Kissinger. It makes sense, then, if you want to learn to pray, go to the expert—Jesus Christ.

No one in history believed more strongly in the power of prayer than Jesus did. No one lived a life of prayer more than Jesus. Only fifty-two days in Jesus' ministry are recorded. But from these snapshots of his life, we see that prayer played an extremely important part.

As mentioned in chapter four, after one very busy day in which Jesus taught in the synagogue, exorcised a demon from a man and healed many people, he got up very early to pray (Mk 1:35); before he chose his twelve disciples, he prayed through the night (Lk 6:12-13); after feeding five thousand men, plus women and children, with only two fish and five small loaves of bread, Jesus went into the hills to pray (Mk 6:46). But also, before his crucifixion, he spent most of the night in prayer. When he found his disciples sleeping in the garden of Gethsemane, he asked, "Could you not keep watch for one hour?" (Mk 14:37). His first and last words on the cross were prayers: "Father, forgive them, for they do not know what they are doing. . . . Father, into your hands I commit my spirit" (Lk 23:34, 46). His final words before his ascension were a prayer (Lk 24:51).

Prayer pervaded Christ's life. He prayed in public and in private. He prayed about ordinary things and crises. He prayed before great decisions and after momentous victories. The life of Christ on earth was prayer. Why should we pray? Because Christ prayed.

The disciples did not fail to notice that Jesus rose early in the morning to pray and stayed up late at night to pray. They recognized the fruit it bore in his life. Never did they find Jesus in a state of panic. So they said to him, "Lord, teach us to pray" (Lk 11:1). In effect, they said, "We want what we see in you. If prayer does so much for you, then we need it all the more."

Jesus was also a man of purpose. He came to do a job. Nothing distracted him from his mission. A sampling of some of his sayings proves my point:

The Son of Man came to seek and to save what was lost. (Lk 19:10)

I have come that they may have life, and have it to the full. (Jn 10:10)

The Son of Man did not come to be served, but to serve, and to give his life as a ransom for many. (Mk 10:45)

I am the good shepherd. The good shepherd lays down his life for the sheep. (Jn 10:11)

The Son of Man must suffer many things and be rejected by the elders, chief priests and teachers of the law, and . . . be killed and after three days rise again. (Mk 8:31)

I lay down my life—only to take it up again. No one takes it from me, but I lay it down of my own accord. I have authority to lay it down and authority to take it up again. (Jn 10:17-18)

Jesus knew that he came to save the lost and give life. He came to lay down his life as a ransom for all humankind. He knew he would be put to death and raised to life three days later. From his earliest days of ministry, he spoke of his determination to go to the cross. It was no coincidence that Jesus was a man of prayer and a man of purpose. The two go together.

If we want to know the purpose for which God called us, we too must be people of prayer. It is through prayer that we sense what God is calling us to do. Not any prayer will do, however. We must look to Jesus to teach us how to pray.

When Jesus' disciples asked him to teach them to pray, he responded with the Lord's Prayer. It is a model for prayer. It is a total prayer. Its concerns embrace the whole world—from the coming of his kingdom to our daily bread. Large things and small things, spiritual things and material things, inward things and outward things— nothing is beyond the purview of this prayer.

The Lord's Prayer can be broken into two parts. If we follow these parts closely when we pray, we will experience guidance in our prayers.

God's Concerns

Jesus begins his prayer by addressing God's concerns:

Our Father in heaven . . . (Mt 6:9)

He instructs us to begin our prayer by addressing God as "Our Father." When we pray "Our Father," we are reminded that we are speaking with a personal God who loves us like a father. He delights when we bring our requests to him.

Then Jesus instructs us to add, "in heaven." This helps us understand that we are not speaking with just any father. God encourages intimacy, but he does not call us into a casual, buddy-buddy relationship. He is the Creator of the universe who resides in heaven. Saying "Our Father in heaven" keeps us in balance. God is immanent yet transcendent, both approachable and high and lifted up.

. . . hallowed be your name,
your kingdom come,

your will be done

on earth as it is in heaven. (Mt 6:9-10)

Jesus teaches us to start our prayers with adoration of God. We are to tell God that we want to praise him. All the great prayers of the Bible begin with adoration. Adoration reminds us what a great God we address. When we remember God's power, it helps us put our own problems in perspective. When we spend time worshiping God, our sense of desperation subsides.

When my wife, Jorie, and I pray together, we always begin with adoration of God. It is not uncommon for us to spend thirty minutes or more in praise to God before we share any of our personal needs. Our praise and thanksgiving ushers us into God's presence. We come to realize how awesome and majestic God is. This focus helps us put our own problems in perspective.

Jesus shows us that powerful prayers begin with requests for things that increase God's honor, kingdom and will. If you want to pray like Jesus prayed, start your prayers with petitions for things that further God's work. Keep God's concerns utmost in your mind. One of the great lessons of the Lord's Prayer is to come to God not need-centered or self-centered, but God-centered and kingdom-centered.

Our tendency, of course, is to reverse the order. We so often begin with our needs, hurts and desires. Sometimes that is not only where we begin but where we end as well. We become so absorbed in our own concerns that we never get around to praying for God's concerns, much less worshiping and adoring him.

Sometimes as I pray for God's name to be hallowed, his kingdom to be extended and his will to be done, I realize that my requests do not fit into God's grand purpose. God cannot grant my request, because I am not asking for what is best. I do not give my children all the things they request of me. If I did, I would not be a good father. So why do we expect God to give us everything we ask of him?

I think of the mornings my four-year-old son, Mark, and I shave together. Mark runs into my bathroom and asks, "Are we going to shave, Daddy?"

I reply, "How old are you?"

"Four," he smiles with an impish grin.

"Four! And you're already shaving? Most boys don't shave until they're sixteen! Are you sure you need a shave? Is your beard long and hairy?"

"Yes," he laughs, repeating this conversation he's had with me before. I put a little extra shaving cream in my hand so there will be enough to put in his hand when I finish lathering my face. He giggles with delight when I wipe the whipped-cream-like foam on his chubby little fingers. He proceeds to rub it all over his face. Sometimes even on his nose, ears, or forehead. While I shave, he dances in front of the mirror.

Do I give him a razor blade when he requests it? Never. I'd be a negligent parent if I granted such a request. I don't give him things by which he could hurt himself. No parent gives a young child a sharp knife or a loaded gun, or allows him or her to play in the medicine chest. Nor does God grant requests he knows will not be good for us. He does not give us things that are not in his will. He is too loving to say yes to such petitions.

Greek mythology contains numerous stories of gods or mortals who made requests of Zeus. Often people lived to regret their requests. Aurora, the goddess of the dawn, fell in love with Tithonus, a mortal youth. Zeus offered her any gift she might choose for her mortal lover. Quite naturally, she asked that he might live forever. But she forgot to ask that he stay young forever. So Tithonus grew older and older and could never die. The request she made, which she thought would be for her best good, turned out to be a curse.

God doesn't work that way. He doesn't say, "That's a terrible request, but I'll grant it just to prove a point." God doesn't grant us petitions that are not good for us. This helps us understand Jesus' promise: "Ask and it will be given to you; seek and you will find; knock and the door will be opened to you. For everyone who asks receives; he who seeks finds; and to him who knocks, the door will be opened" (Mt 7:7-8).

This is not an unconditional promise whereby we can expect to receive whatever we request. Jesus lays down some parameters in the next few verses: "Which of you, if his son asks for bread, will give him a stone? Or if he asks for a fish, will give him a snake? If you, then, though you are evil, know how to give good gifts to your children, how much more will your Father in heaven give good gifts to those who ask him!" (Mt 7:9-11).

When we pray for God's concerns before our own, often it helps us recognize that it may not be the right timing for God to grant our request. God is happy to grant what we request, but perhaps he tells us to wait or slow down. Possibly he knows that by granting the petition at a later time, he will receive more glory. If he waits until the situation becomes humanly impossible, he will receive greater honor.

Sometimes God knows we are not yet prepared for what we have asked. He recognizes that the granting of some petitions would corrupt or even harm us. In such cases, it is God's grace and mercy that prevent our prayers from being answered. God withholds his gifts from us for our good. In those cases, we could not handle what might come if our requests were granted.

Praying for God's concerns puts our requests in perspective. It helps us determine when our requests may not be good or at the right time. When we pray for God's kingdom, we make his agenda our agenda. The key to praying with confidence is to ask for things that are in God's will. Praying for God's priorities allows God to bend our desires so that his concerns become our concerns. Then we are on praying ground. Then we are not asking that God bless what we do but that we do what God blesses. We are praying to do God's will rather than that he approve our will.

Bobby Richardson, former New York Yankees second baseman, prayed at a meeting of the Fellowship of Christian Athletes: "Dear God, your will, nothing more, nothing less, nothing else. Amen." If we pray like that, our prayers will be shorter . . . and better. We will be asking for things that further God's kingdom and that are good for us.

So what is God's will for us? We have already seen that God wants us to know Christ, become conformed to the image of Christ and share Christ. God wants to transform our lives so that we become more and more like Christ. Then we exude the fragrance of Christ and attract others to him. This gives us all kinds of opportunities to testify about the difference Christ is making in our lives. As we share Christ with other people and invite them to church with us, we are helping God's kingdom come, for we are extending God's kingdom among our friends and associates.

We cannot pray "your kingdom come" unless we are willing to be part of the answer by spreading God's kingdom. Whenever we pray, we must be ready for God to use us as part of the answer. We find guidance when we make God's concerns our top priority. When God sees that his honor, will and kingdom are our top priority, then he is able to show us his purposes in the world and how we can become part of fulfilling them.

Our Concerns

God doesn't want us to limit our prayers to his concerns. He knows that we also have all kinds of personal needs. So Jesus instructs us to continue our prayer:

Give us today our daily bread.

Forgive us our debts,

as we also have forgiven our debtors.

And lead us not into temptation,

but deliver us from the evil one. (Mt 6:11-13)

These requests cover all our needs—our material, spiritual, and moral needs. It is striking to move from praying about God's kingdom to asking for daily bread. Some find it unthinkable that God would trouble himself with our concerns for daily bread. If it had come from the lips of any other than Jesus himself, we would consider it an intrusion of materialism upon the refined realm of prayer. But God wants us to share with him every detail of our needs. Nothing is too small for him to be interested in. If it's big enough for us to worry about, it is important enough for God to listen to. He wants us to depend on him for everything.

Aleksandr Solzhenitsyn, in a fictionalized account of his experience in the Russian Gulag, tells of making a very specific request of God. His alter ego, Ivan Denisovich, stood in line for inspection at the end of the day. He had no fear because he had nothing to conceal. Although he couldn't remember having anything forbidden, eight years in camp had given him the habit of caution. So he thrust a hand into his pants pocket to make sure it was empty.

And there lay a small piece of broken hacksaw blade, the tiny length of steel that he'd picked up in his thriftiness at the building site without any intention of bringing it to camp. Prisoners, of course, were not allowed such implements in their prison cells. An urgent prayer rose in his heart: "Oh Lord, save me. Don't let them send me to the cells." For that strip of hacksaw he could get ten days in solitary confinement. Quickly he stuffed it into his left mitten.

While all this raced through his mind, the guard, after finishing the right-hand mitten, stretched a hand to deal with the left. Just then, the guard heard his chief, who was in a hurry to get on, shout to the escort: "Come on, bring up the machine-works column." Instead of examining the other mitten, the old guard waved on Denisovich. Thus the prisoner learned that God is interested in the smallest details of our lives.[1]

How about you? Do your requests cover every need in your life? Or do you only bring to God the presidential decisions? Jesus' example should be enough to assure us that he doesn't want us to seek his guidance only on big decisions such as the choice of a college, vocation or mate. He wants us to ask him for guidance in the daily, mundane decisions as well.

How do we reconcile Jesus' teaching that we are to bring before him our daily needs with the freedom to choose whatever we think best as long as we remain within God's grand design (discussed in chapter two)? Although we have freedom to make choices within God's grand design, we are still to share with God all our concerns. Even though God has given us wisdom to make decisions on our own, he is concerned with even the smallest of our needs and wants us to pray about them.

Our material needs. When Jesus tell us to pray "Give us this day our daily bread," he makes clear that God wants us to ask for our material needs. God is not interested only in our spiritual needs. He wants us to bring him our concerns about our daily provisions.

A family in Dallas sold their business to enter vocational Christian work. Things got rough. Finally they were in desperate need of food and clothing. One night at family worship, after the mother asked if there were any requests, little Timmy said, "Mommy, do you think

Jesus would mind if I asked for a shirt?" She wrote down "shirt for Timmy" in the book where they recorded requests and answers and added "size 7."

So every night Timmy implored, "Don't forget, Mommy, pray for the shirt." And every night they did.

One day as the mother was working around the house, she got a telephone call from a clothier in downtown Dallas. "I am just completing our July clearance sale," he said, "and I've got some shirts left over. You've got four boys; it occurred to me that you might be able to use some."

"What size?" she asked.

"Size 7."

"How many?"

"Twelve. Could you use them?"

Most of us in this position would have taken the shirts, stuffed them in a drawer, made some casual comment, and that would be it. Not this wise parent. That night, as she expected, little Timmy said, "Mommy, don't forget to pray for the shirt."

"No, Timmy," she said, "we can thank the Lord; he answered our prayer."

"He did?" Little Timmy's eyes went wide. As previously arranged, Tommy, the older boy, went out, got a shirt, brought it in and put it down on the table. He went out, got another shirt and brought it back. Out and back—twelve times! One little boy in Dallas knows God cares enough to answer our prayers, even prayers about a shirt.

It should not surprise us that God cares about meeting our daily needs. This is completely consistent with Jesus' pattern of living, for he occupied himself with the so-called trivialities of humankind. He provided wine for a wedding party, food for those who were hungry and rest for those who were weary (Jn 2:1-12; 6:1-14; Mk 6:31).

Try to imagine what our prayer experience would be like if he had forbidden us to ask for the little things. What if the only things we were allowed to talk about were the weighty matters? We would have to exclude God from the bulk of our day, for most of our time is spent with mundane matters. But God does care when we lose our keys, can't find a baby sitter, suffer from a headache or don't know if we can make ends meet. So bring all your needs to God in prayer.

God loves to meet our needs beyond our wildest expectations—with one condition. We must ask. Not only are we to bring our needs to God, but we need to make our requests specific.

Why is it important that our requests be specific? Because God is most apt to answer prayers when he will receive glory. Only when we make specific requests does it become clear that God has answered. Only when we make specific requests are we likely to give him the praise. When we make a general petition such as "God, bless our family," how do we know when God has intervened on our behalf? But when we ask God to provide us with a precise amount of money to cover all our expenses this month, it is easy to determine if God answered our prayer.

Years ago, I learned there's power in prayer when you pray specifically in public. To ask God in public to do something is to take the risk of others' knowing my prayer was not answered.

When Jorie and I worked in youth ministry, Jorie sat down with one of the Christian high-school girls before one of our weekend trips and asked, "Marcia, how many sophomore girls would you like to see come on the weekend? How many girls do you think God could help us get on this retreat?"

Marcia said, "Let's pray for twelve." So they asked God for twelve. They prayed. They talked to girls. They made calls. Friday night, as the retreat began, Jorie and Marcia spent a rare moment alone in their cabin. Marcia said to Jorie, "Do you know how many sophomore girls we have in our cabin?" They counted the sleeping bags in the room. Sure enough, with God's help they had gotten twelve girls to come. Marcia was so excited. God had answered their prayers. God wants us to risk being publicly specific with our prayers.

Our spiritual needs. Jesus moves from our material needs to praying for our spiritual needs: "Forgive us our debts." We ask God to forgive our sins. Just as with our other requests, our confessions need to be specific. When I lump all my sins together and confess them en masse, it's neither painful nor embarrassing. But if I admit my wrongs one at a time and call them by name, I am far more likely to experience God's cleansing forgiveness and gain victory over these individual sins.

This is the one petition in his prayer that Jesus presents as a conditional request: "Forgive us our debts, as we also have forgiven our debtors." We are forgiven as we forgive. And, as if to intensify the problem, this is the only petition that Jesus feels compelled to enlarge upon later: "For if you forgive men when they sin against you, your heavenly Father will also forgive you. But if you do not forgive men their sins, your Father will not forgive your sins" (Mt 6:14-15).

If I don't forgive others, it indicates that I haven't been humbled before God. If I have been humbled by my sins, I will be lenient toward others. When we ask God to forgive us and to help us graciously forgive others, we are asking him to change us and our attitudes toward other people.

On February 17, 1985, some four hundred men and women gathered to pray in St. Patrick's Church in Canonsburg, Pennsylvania. The McGraw-Edison Company had told its employees that without a considerable "giveback" in wages and benefits the company would close down its Canonsburg plant. When the union leadership responded to the ultimatum with a resounding no, the likelihood of a shutdown increased. The impact on the town would be disastrous.

The Reverend David Kinsey, chairman of the Canonsburg Ministerial Association, the ministers of the town, labor and management personnel from McGraw-Edison, their families and a large ecumenical group of praying people gathered to ask God to change hearts and change history. At the climax of that prayer rally, Wayne T. Alderson, a Christian labor relations and management consultant and founder of Value of the Person, Inc., asked the senior management representative for McGraw-Edison and the president of the local United Steel Workers Union to come and stand with him at the front of the church. What a sight to behold in the beleaguered town of Canonsburg!

The labor leader prayed for McGraw-Edison management, and the manager prayed for the trade union leaders and membership. The result: two days later management changed its offer (though there was still to be a reduction in salary and benefits), and the labor force changed its vote. Praying people had changed the history of Canonsburg and McGraw-Edison.[2]

A willingness to forgive people who have wronged us shows that we recognize how much God has forgiven us. An unwillingness to cut other people some slack suggests that we do not really fathom the extent of God's graciousness toward us.

How about you? Is there someone you need to forgive? Someone who was cruel and hurt you deeply? Stop right now and ask God to help you forgive. God cannot guide you into any deeper understanding of his will until you obey the truths he has already shown you.

Our moral needs. Finally, Jesus moves to praying for our moral needs: "And lead us not into temptation, but deliver us from the evil one." What does Jesus mean, "Lead us not into temptation?" Certainly, God would not lead us into sin, would he? No, of course not.

James writes, "When tempted, no one should say, 'God is tempting me.' For God cannot be tempted by evil, nor does he tempt anyone; but each one is tempted when, by his own evil desire, he is dragged away and enticed" (Jas 1:13-14). We are tempted by our own desires. These desires in our heart are the seeds of destruction. God does not tempt us.

So what does Jesus mean? Jesus is suggesting that we ask God to remove the evil desires from our hearts so that he will not have to test our hearts. Judas had a problem with money, which was precisely why Jesus made him the treasurer of the apostolic band—so that what was in his heart would come to light. The prayer "lead us not into temptation" means "Lord, may there be nothing in me that will force you to put me to the test in order to reveal what is in my heart."

When we pray "deliver us from the evil one," we admit that there is a kingdom of evil at work in the world. Why do Christians so often get discouraged and depressed? Why do husbands and wives struggle with each other? Why are children prone to rebel against authority? Why do churches face dissension? Why do so many things go from bad to worse? Because Satan wants to destroy Christians, marriages, families and churches.

We acknowledge that the devil is strong and we need our heavenly Father to deliver us. We need God's strength to keep us from falling to temptation. When we pray this request, we are asking God to give us the courage to claim our Christ-given authority to drive out and bind the spiritual forces of evil. Gaining victory over our enemy is such an important part of God's will for us that I devote the entire next chapter to discernment in dealing with Satan.

We must pray for deliverance from the evil one for ourselves and our brothers and sisters in Christ. Without these prayers, we become easy prey for the enemy. The Reverend Ron Dunn had a particularly difficult year in his church and his ministry. He tells this story:

One summer I took my family to the south coast of Texas, thinking that the gentle rhythm of the waves sliding back and forth across the Gulf Coast beaches might wash a little calm into our souls.

It had not been a good year and it was only half over. A few days before we left, our youngest son added variety to the situation by breaking his leg.

He now wore a cast from his hip to his toes. The x-rays showed not only the break but some tumor-like growths on the bone. Too soon yet to know what they were. I used my imagination.

So there we were, soaking up the sun and surf at in-season rates. And every morning when I woke up, there he was, my gloomy companion: depression. He was waiting for me beside the bed—the waves had not washed him away. I couldn't shake him. We went everywhere together, me and my shadow.

Until Thursday morning. I woke up and he wasn't there. I was suspicious. All day long I expected him to leap out from some dark alley, but there wasn't a sign of him. I relaxed from the inside out. Not a single thing had changed but everything was different.

Back home a few days later, I went to my office to pick up the mail that had piled up while I was away. One of the letters bore an unfamiliar hotel logo but I recognized the handwriting. It was from a friend who knew everything about my situation. Next to the date was the time the letter had been written: 3 A.M.

Dear Ron . . .

I have prayed for you today and am about to pray again that God will make this time through which you are passing a new door open to the mystery of truth. God must love you so much to watch you pass through this trying time. . . .

So, no sermons at this point. I am going to say the thing that means the most to me at this moment with reference to you. I have no friend on the face of the earth whose friendship I treasure more than yours. I have asked God to put on my heart as much burden as He can to lighten yours. I want to bear it with you. That does not require conversation or correspondence. But in the spiritual realm where those transactions are made, I have asked God for your burden. . . .

I was not surprised to see that the date on the letter was the Thursday I awoke without my sepulchral companion waiting for me.[3]

Is this what Paul had in mind when he told us to bear one another's burdens? This is surely what T. DeWitt Talmadge had in mind when he said, "The mightiest thing you can do for a man is to pray for him." Do you believe you can do nothing greater for a person than to pray for him or her? Do you know that your prayers can deliver friends from the snares of the evil one?

Summing Up

We have come to the right place to learn how to pray for guidance. Jesus is the master teacher. His prayer is perfectly balanced with God's concerns and our concerns. His prayer covers everything—material, spiritual and moral needs. He leaves us a good model to follow. If our top priority is to pray for God's concerns, then God will gladly guide us into what he wants us to do and promises to meet all our personal needs. He leaves us a good example to follow, for we need guidance in our material, spiritual and moral needs. It's a total prayer for total guidance.

Questions for Reflection and Discussion

1. Jesus is God the Son. He was God incarnate. Why did he need to pray or choose to pray?

2. Why is it important that we begin our prayer by calling God "Father"?

What does that tell us about our relationship with him and his willingness to answer our prayers?

3. Why is it important for our prayers to begin with God's concerns? How does this help us?

How much time do you devote to praising God and praying about his concerns?

4. Jesus also instructs us to pray about our own concerns. Does it surprise you that he teaches us to pray about such minute details as "our daily bread"? Why does God want us to pray about all the details in our lives?

5. Why is it helpful to be publicly specific in our prayers? Is this your practice?

6. What principle or insight was most helpful to you in this chapter?

SIX

Praying for
Discernment
in Dealing with
the Enemy

♦

I HAVE a confession to make. I have not always understood the importance of prayer. Do you know the picture I get when I think about prayer? I imagine myself as a chaplain in the U.S. Army. I am standing before President George Bush in January 1991, pleading with him to let me join General H. Norman Schwarzkopf Jr. and the 320,000 U.S. Army and Marine ground soldiers readied for battle in Saudi Arabia. If Iraq fails to withdraw from Kuwait by the January 15 deadline set by the U.N. Security Council, I want to go in with the Navy and Air Force personnel who are poised to launch the most dramatic air attack in history.

"You are courageous, pastor," Bush replies, "but it will be dangerous. You had better stay here where it's safe."

"But I want to help," I reply.

The president's eyes fasten on me. "You can pray."

January 15 comes and goes. Saddam Hussein and the Iraqi military ignore the withdrawal ultimatum. Suddenly, the Allied forces launch an air attack at 3:00 a.m. January 17 in and around Baghdad. The world watches forty-two days of air bombardment, which includes 110,000 combat sorties (individual bombing missions) and a one-hundred-hour ground war, which smashes what had been the largest army in the Middle East in the most lopsided victory in modern military history.

The camera of my imagination does not follow me into the chapel to pray. It chases after Schwarzkopf and the Allied forces. That's where the action is.

Let's admit it. Prayer suffers from a poor image. Some people dismiss prayer as a weak alternative to practical action, an alibi for doing nothing. Prayer is fine if there's nothing else you can do, but the real action is on the front lines.

My attitude toward prayer has changed dramatically in recent years. So much so that when one of our members told me that he was one of only two people who gathered in our prayer room to pray during the 8:00 service on Easter Sunday, I thanked him for praying and assured him that he was doing the most important work on our church campus. We tend to think that the most important work is done by the minister of music who leads the choir and congregation in worship or the preacher who proclaims the message. I no longer believe that. The most fundamental and significant work is done when we pray.

Where's the Battle?

We are never more in God's will than when we pray. We are never closer to finding God's will for our lives than when we pray. Any things or forces that keep us from prayer must be regarded as enemies. If you need some convincing, look with me at the apostle Paul's words:

> Put on the full armor of God so that you can take your stand against the devil's schemes. For our struggle is not against flesh and blood, but against the rulers, against the authorities, against the powers

of this dark world and against the spiritual forces of evil in the heavenly realms. Therefore put on the full armor of God, so that when the day of evil comes, you may be able to stand your ground, and after you have done everything, to stand. Stand firm then, with the belt of truth buckled around your waist, with the breastplate of righteousness in place, and with your feet fitted with the readiness that comes from the gospel of peace. In addition to all this, take up the shield of faith, with which you can extinguish all the flaming arrows of the evil one. Take the helmet of salvation and the sword of the Spirit, which is the word of God. (Eph 6:11-17)

Follow what Paul is saying closely. He tells us there is a spiritual war requiring spiritual equipment. Then he tells us to suit up for the fight—put on the whole armor of God. So you say, "All right, here I am, Paul; I'm dressed and ready to go. I have on the helmet of salvation. I'm holding the shield of faith. The sword of the Spirit is in my other hand. The belt of truth is strapped to my waist. The breastplate of righteousness protects my torso. Now where's the war? I'm ready to fight; point me in the direction of the battle."

And he does: "Pray in the Spirit on all occasions with all kinds of prayers and requests. With this in mind, be alert and always keep on praying for all the saints" (Eph 6:18). Is he serious? I've made intense preparation, I'm wearing an iron suit that weighs a ton and am wielding this giant sword, and what does Paul tell me to do? Pray. Where's the battle? In the prayer room. That's the battlefield upon which the spiritual war is waged. The battle is won or lost there. Before we ever step onto the battlefield of preaching or teaching or witnessing, the outcome has already been determined on the battlefield of prayer.[1]

Scripture records a battle the Israelites waged with the Amalekites in Exodus 17. Moses told Joshua to lead the soldiers into the valley to fight, and he'd get on top of the mountain and hold up the rod of God. A strange thing happened. When Moses held up the rod, Joshua prevailed; when he lowered the rod, Amalek prevailed. After a while Moses grew tired, and his hands became lead weights. Seeing the divine connection, Aaron and Hur held up Moses' arms so that Joshua could prevail.

Where was the battle decided? In the valley with Joshua? No, it was decided on the mountain with Moses. The victory in the valley was won by the intercession on the mountain. The church could win more battles in the valley if it had more intercessors on the mountain lifting high the name of Jesus.

J. O. Frasier left England many years ago to bring the message of Christ's love to the Lisus—unreached tribes who lived in the high mountain ranges of western China. The entry to the ranges was at their midpoint, the site of a small outpost village. One tribe lived to the north of the village, the other to the south.

Frasier realized that he would probably be the only missionary to this tribe for years to come. He prayed, "Lord, which way should I go? North or south?" His Master said, "Both. Pray for the Southern Lisus from sunup to noon and evangelize the Northern Lisus from noon to sundown."

This became the pattern of his life for years. He prayed for half the day for Lisus in the south he had never met and evangelized the Northern Lisu tribal groups around him. The work grew slowly. A few hundred Christians were the harvest of a decade.

After many years, he left the field for the first time to rest and get supplies in the outpost village. Now very familiar with the tribal tongue, he heard a Lisu speaking with a different dialect in the market. He had met his first Southern Lisu! Lovingly, Frasier invited the man to come and stay with him in his rented quarters. As he heard the message of Jesus, the Lisu was quick to respond and accept him as his Lord and Savior.

For several weeks, Frasier tutored the illiterate man, helping him to memorize passages of Scripture. He told him story after story from the Bible, always praying that the Spirit would sharpen his ability to remember what he was hearing. As the men parted, Frasier urged him to tell all the Southern Lisus about Jesus. He then returned to the site of his own ministry, praying as usual for half of each day for those to the south.

Years passed. Then one day a delegation of Southern Lisus arrived at his village. They reported that thousands of Southern Lisus had followed Christ and were in desperate need of someone to teach them more! As tears of joy welled up in his eyes, the missionary realized his time invested in prayer from sunup to noon had caused a harvest hundreds of times greater than all his labors from noon to sundown. It was as though God were saying, "Not by might, nor by power, but by my Spirit, shall the Lisus be reached."[2] Don't forget it. In God's work, the primary battlefield is in the field of prayer.

We are studying how you and I can discern God's will for our lives. Let me underscore this point. It is God's will that you be a person of prayer. Prayer is one of the foremost spiritual weapons God has given you to defeat the enemy. If you are not praying, you are out of God's will. If you are not praying regularly for your family members, your pastor, your government leaders and the friends you want to come to Christ, you are not fulfilling God's will for you.

Who Is the Enemy?

If the most significant battle is engaged in prayer, who is the enemy? Paul tells us our struggle is not against flesh and blood but against the spiritual forces of evil in the heavenly realms (Eph 6:12).

When you face problems, you may think your battle is against fellow human beings. But Paul says there's more to your enemy than meets the eye. Your real battle is with the spiritual forces of evil. When people read this for the first time, they are usually amazed—surprised to learn of an unseen world of angels and demons out there. Your children, right now, are being watched over by angels. I'm willing to wager that the angel who watches over our four-year-old has had three nervous breakdowns.

The primary target in prayer is not the person or problem you face but the powers behind these troubles. Too few Christians recognize that much of prayer is a power encounter with the spiritual forces of evil. We find one of the clearest examples of this in Daniel.

Daniel has been praying for twenty-one days for God to bring back the people of Judah from the Babylonian captivity, living under the rule of the Persians. An angel appears to him and brings this message:

> Do not be afraid, Daniel. Since the first day that you set your mind to gain understanding and to humble yourself before your God, your words were heard, and I have come in response to them. But the prince of the Persian kingdom resisted me twenty-one days.

Then Michael, one of the chief princes, came to help me, because I
was detained there with the king of Persia. (Dan 10:12-13)

Who is this prince? Some have argued that this refers to the king of
Persia. But Hebrew has another word for "king." Furthermore, it is
highly unlikely that a man would furnish an angel of God sufficient
opposition to detain the angel for twenty-one days. If one angel was able
to smite 185,000 Assyrians in one night in the days of Hezekiah, no
human being could detain an angel. The thought here is of spiritual
warfare. Israel has an angelic "prince," Michael; hence, it is to be expected
that the prince of Persia should also be an angel, that is, the supernatural
spiritual power standing behind the national gods. A bad angel, called a
demon in the New Testament, is, without a doubt, referred to here.
Daniel's prayer was heard immediately, and an answer was dispatched
by God. But a demonic force, apparently of a rank greater than that of
the angelic messenger, intercepted the message.

Daniel tells us more of the angel's message: "So he said, 'Do you
know why I have come to you? Soon I will return to fight against the
prince of Persia, and when I go, the prince of Greece will come'" (Dan
10:20). If there is a demonic prince of Persia and of Greece, this implies
that every nation is tormented or dominated by some such prince.
There must be demonic princes who rule over Egypt, China and
America. Powerful forces of evil are at work in and through the
nations and their rulers to defeat and overthrow the people of God.

Bill Jackson tells in *World Christian* magazine of a missionary couple
in Thailand who saw no fruit for years until they decided to set one
day a week aside to go into the woods and oppose the territorial spirits
in prayer warfare. A wave of conversions followed. Jackson believes
that thousands of unreached people are currently under the thumb of
Satan, and "the gospel won't go forward among these peoples until
we bind the spirits that bind them, whether these deceptive forces be
Islam, Hinduism, or any of a myriad of others."[3]

We cannot simply pray for people. We must pray against the
powers who hold them in bondage. They are the real enemy.

What Is the Enemy Like?

If we are to be prepared for this battle, we must take stock of our enemy. So we ask, What are the characteristics of these spiritual forces of evil? In Ephesians 6:11-12, Paul cites four characteristics.

First, they are real. If we deny the existence of these spiritual forces of evil, we will see no need for God's armor, will enter the conflict unarmed and will be quickly and decisively defeated.

A helpful documentary about the reality of the demonic came in the early 1970s movie *The Exorcist*. Many viewers casually dismissed it as Hollywood sensationalism, but it was actually an accurate portrayal of demon possession. It was based on a historical account of a demon-possessed child in Georgetown, a wealthy residential district in Washington, D.C. The hesitancy of the scientific community to admit to demonic reality was effectively portrayed: obvious poltergeistic activity was explained away as "muscular spasms." The characteristics of demon possession (sex fixation, self-mutilation, vomiting, violence to others, gross language, multiple voices, supernatural strength and knowledge) were thought to be schizophrenia. Only when it became obvious that internists and psychiatrists could do nothing for her daughter did the mother turn to the church. Finally she had to admit that her daughter had spiritual problems. She discovered the reality of the demonic.

We find similar descriptions of demon-possessed people when we look at some of Jesus' encounters with the demonic. You will find the characteristics of the people Jesus exorcised much like the girl described in the movie. The demoniac in Mark 5:1-20 exhibited a violent disposition and supernatural strength and practiced self-mutilation. The demon-possessed boy in Mark 9:14-29 had frequent convulsions and displayed self-destructive behavior.

Second, they are cunning. Paul tells us that these spiritual forces have "schemes." We need to be prepared for the cunning methods of the devil. He seldom attacks openly. The devil and his demonic horde are so subtle that most people are not even aware of them.

Third, they are powerful. Paul tells us they are "rulers." They are "authorities." They are "world powers." They control people and entire governments.

Fourth, they are wicked. The apostle warns us that they are "spiritual forces of evil." They have no morals and pursue malicious designs. Their intentions are never good.

How Can You and I Defeat the Enemy?

Having learned of these terrible creatures, you may wonder: Is there any hope for us? Are we any match for them? If so, how can you and I defeat these spiritual enemies? The good news is that Jesus Christ has far more power than these spiritual forces of evil and has prevailed over them: "Having disarmed the powers and authorities, he made a public spectacle of them, triumphing over them by the cross" (Col 2:15). Through his death and resurrection, Christ defeated their two weapons: sin and death. Now, as we rely on Christ and pray in the power of his name, we are more than a match for our enemies.

In 2 Corinthians 10:3-4, Paul tells us that we must rely on prayer to do battle with the spiritual forces of evil: "For though we live in the world, we do not wage war as the world does. The weapons we fight with are not the weapons of the world. On the contrary, they have divine power to demolish strongholds." Since we are fighting with a spiritual enemy, we must use spiritual weapons.

We read earlier in Ephesians 6 that the primary weapon of Christian warfare is prayer. It is the secret weapon of the kingdom. It is like a missile that can be fired toward any spot on earth, travel undetected at the speed of thought and hit its target every time. What's more, Satan has no defense against this weapon; he does not have an antiprayer missile. Unbelievers have many defenses against our evangelistic efforts. They can refuse to attend church. Hand them a Bible or Christian book, and they can ignore it. Get on TV, and they can switch channels. Call them on the phone, and they can hang up. But they cannot prevent Christ from knocking at the door of their heart in response to our intercession. People we cannot reach any other way can be reached by way of prayer.

In one scene in Frank Perretti's book *Piercing the Darkness*, God's angels are dismayed by the quantity of demons dropping out of the sky all around them.

Then suddenly, all around the motel, such an unexpected legion of harassing demons began to shower down that Chimon and Scion could no longer hide and had to throw any subtlety to the wind. They were in full glory, bright and visible, swatting and slashing as the demons swarmed around them like vile, biting bees. The intensity of the onslaught was shocking, surprisingly strong. It seemed each spirit would be swatted away only to be replaced by two more, and the air was filled with them. They were bold, brash, reckless, attacking with screams and shrieks, even grinning mockingly.

"For Destroyer!" they screamed as their battle cry. "For Destroyer!"

So that was it. The demonic warlord was trying a new tactic now, and this difficulty could only be caused by one thing: something had happened to their prayer cover.[4]

The demonic forces made their presence known because Christians were not praying. On the other hand, when believers prayed in *This Present Darkness,* the spiritual forces of evil were pushed back and dismayed, while God's angelic forces were strengthened in power and number.

Countless [good] spirits were arriving in the town of Ashton. . . . They rushed in under the ground, they filtered in under the cover of occasional clouds, they sneaked in by riding invisibly in cars, trucks, vans, buses. In hiding places all over the town one warrior would be joined by another, those two would be joined by two more, those four would be joined by four. They too could hear the singing. They could feel the strength coursing through them with every note. Their swords droned with the resonance of the worship. It was the worship and the prayers of these saints that had called them here in the first place.[5]

Could it be that the dull and lifeless worship we experience in many of our churches is due to a lack of prayer? Might one reason so many believers feel an uncertainty about God's will for their lives be because they fail to pray? Are the defeat and lack of power experienced by so many Christian ministries symptoms of prayerlessness? If we give ourselves to heartfelt prayer, we can expect our ministries to grow in vibrancy and effectiveness. We have no reason to be afraid of Satan and his emissaries, for the One who is in us is greater than the one who is in the world (1 Jn 4:4).

One of my favorite passages is 2 Kings 6. The king of Aram was at war with Israel, but whatever he tried militarily, he was outwitted by the king of Israel. The king of Aram decided that one of his men was a traitor, giving away his military secrets. His officers said, "No, it is not us, but it is Elisha, the prophet who is in Israel. He tells the king the very words you speak in your bedroom." So the king sent a strong military force to capture Elisha. They surrounded the city (see vv. 9-14).

When they arrived, Elisha's servant was frightened and bewildered by the huge army that encircled them. "What shall we do?" he cried to Elisha.

"Don't be afraid," the prophet answered. "Those who are with us are more than those who are with them."

And Elisha prayed, "O Lord, open his eyes so he may see." Then the Lord opened the servant's eyes, and he looked and saw the hills full of horses and chariots of fire all around Elisha (vv. 16-17).

My prayer is that as you read this book you will give yourself more to prayer, that as you do so, you will gain confidence that God's forces are greater than the ones who are in the world, and that you will experience a certainty about God's will for your life. If we are to defeat the powers of evil that cause discord and dissension among us, and if we are to reach our neighbors, friends and family members who are held in bondage to Satan, we simply must become a praying people. Your church and mine will have to give themselves to prayer. When we do not pray, the demonic forces laugh at our efforts. But when we pray, strongholds are broken, and the church experiences power.

Five young college students were spending a Sunday in London, so they went to hear the famed C. H. Spurgeon preach. While waiting for the doors to open, the students were greeted by a man who said, "Gentlemen, let me show you around. Would you like to see the heating plant of this church?" They were not particularly interested, for it was a hot day in July. But they didn't want to offend the stranger, so they consented. The young men were taken down a stairway, a door was quietly opened, and the guide whispered, "This is our heating plant." Surprised, the students saw seven hundred people bowed in prayer, seeking a blessing on the service that was soon to begin in the auditorium above. Softly closing the door, the man then introduced himself. It was none other than Charles Spurgeon.

With such an army of prayer warriors undergirding his ministry, is it any wonder that he wielded the sword of the Spirit with such power and effectiveness? Spurgeon credited his success to his praying church members. Years later he declared, "Among all the formative influences that go to make up a man honored of God in the ministry, I know of none more mighty than the intercession of his parishioners. Without it he will most likely be a failure!"

The Last Word

Since prayer puts us in the center of God's will and is essential to discovering God's will, you can be certain that the spiritual forces of evil will do everything in their power to keep us from prayer. Try a little experiment. Next time you set aside time to pray, count the number of interruptions that occur to keep you from prayer. A phone call, a pressing problem that you must deal with immediately, a sudden recall of something you forgot to do, a family member who needs to talk, a TV program—you could add a hundred other things that call a halt to your prayers. I am well aware that we are the ones who make the choice to let these distractions keep us from prayer. But make no mistake that Satan will send dozens of thoughts your way to take your focus off prayer. He will do everything in his power to confuse you and remove the thought of prayer from your mind so that you will not make wise decisions.

Did you realize that prayer must be at the center of your life? It must be the very foundation of your church. It is where the battle is won or lost in every work of God. Is it the bedrock foundation of your church? Your ministry? Your life? Seeing anew the importance of prayer, will you commit yourself to praying more this week? Will you covenant to help develop a "heating plant" in your church or ministry, or join one that already exists? Prayer is the primary weapon Christ has given us to push back the spiritual forces of evil.

Questions for Reflection and Discussion

1. How do you identify with Ron when he confesses that he has not

always understood the importance of prayer?

How have you shared the belief of many Christians that preaching and teaching, leading worship, witnessing and building relationships with unbelievers are more important than prayer?

2. Why does Ron suggest that our most fundamental and significant work is done when we pray?

Why does he suggest that we must engage in prayer first before we engage in any other efforts for God's kingdom?

3. Reflect on the experience of J. O. Frasier. More people came to Christ among the Southern Lisus for whom he prayed than among the Northern Lisus among whom he worked. What does this tell you about the power in prayer?

4. Read Ephesians 6:11-12. Reflect on some of the opposition, obstacles and difficulties with people you face in your life and in ministries in which you are engaged. Do you believe that Satanic forces play a significant role in your troubles? Why or why not?

5. Read Daniel 10:12-13, 20. Do you believe that demonic forces have the power to detain our prayers and to limit the success of the gospel in various regions around the world? How can we overcome their power?

6. What principle or insight in this chapter was most helpful to you?

SEVEN

The Importance of Praise in Obtaining Guidance

◆

A MAN was confined to a hospital room for many months with heart disease and numerous medical complications. His condition was so delicate that he had to be partially quarantined. While there, he made a little wooden truck for his young boy.

When the boy's birthday came, he visited the hospital. The youngster was not allowed to go up to see his father on the fifth floor, nor was the father allowed to come down, so an orderly, dressed in white, delivered the carefully crafted truck. The father stood at the window watching the orderly give the child the present. The boy opened it, found the truck and jumped for joy. Then he leaped into the orderly's arms and hugged and kissed him. Meanwhile, his father was waving at the window, trying to get his son's attention: "Hey, I was the one who made that truck!"

Finally his wife and the orderly showed the youth his father standing at the window. When the boy saw his father, he cried, "Oh, thank you, Daddy! I love you. I miss you. Come home."

How like the child of God. We become so enamored with the gifts God has given us that we forget the Giver. We enjoy the home, the food, the vacation; we take pleasure with the friends, the ministry and the job; but we easily forget that it is God who gave them to us. God wants us to look up and say, "Thank you, Lord."

Under the inspiration of the Holy Spirit, Paul writes, "Give thanks in all circumstances, for this is God's will for you in Christ Jesus" (1 Thess 5:18). It is God's will that we be thankful people. The writer to the Hebrews penned, "Through Jesus, therefore, let us continually offer to God a sacrifice of praise—the fruit of lips that confess his name" (Heb 13:15). It is God's will that we be thankful and filled with praise.

How much time do you spend thanking God for all he has given you? How often do you express gratitude for what God is doing in your life, your family and in your church? What portion of your prayers is devoted to praising God? Praise and thanksgiving are two sides to what we call prayers of adoration. The usual distinction between these two experiences is this: in praise we give glory to God for who he is; in thanksgiving we give glory to God for what he has done for us.

If you're like most people, you probably fail to praise God like you should. Most mornings when I awake, I have to drag myself out of bed. I've modeled this behavior to my entire family, so we are a family of night owls. When I wake up our six kids in the morning, they all groan and struggle to get their bodies jump-started. We identify with the eleven-year-old girl who wrote a letter to her pastor.

Dear Pastor,

We say grace at our house before every meal except at breakfast. Nobody talks at breakfast.

We have to work at praising God, especially in the morning. Grumbling comes naturally for us, but we have to work at praise and thanksgiving. It is worth the effort, however, for it is God's design that we praise him. If we want to know God's will and obtain his guidance, we must learn to be praisers.

Reasons to Praise

Why is it God's will that we be praisers? Why are the prayers of the saints in the Bible filled with praise to God? Why are there so many psalms of praise and thanksgiving in the psalter? I can think of at least four reasons why an attitude of praise puts us in the center of God's will and increases the likelihood of us obtaining further guidance into God's grand design for us.

First, praise is God's will. Scripture commands us to praise God. Paul says, "Rejoice in the Lord always; again I will say, rejoice!" (Phil 4:4 NASB). In 1 Thessalonians 5:16 he writes, "Rejoice always" (NASB). Because of what Christ did for us, praise should characterize our lives:

Praise the LORD.

Praise, O servants of the LORD,

 praise the name of the LORD.

Let the name of the LORD be praised,

 both now and forevermore.

From the rising of the sun to the place where it sets,

 the name of the LORD is to be praised. (Ps 113:1-3)

God loves to receive our praise and thanksgiving. Like the proud mother who is thrilled to receive a wilted bouquet of dandelions from her child, so God celebrates our feeble attempts at praise.

The first question in the Presbyterian Church's Shorter Catechism reads, "What is the chief end of man?" Answer: "Man's chief end is to glorify God, and to enjoy Him forever." Our purpose is not just to obey God or serve him or witness about him, but to enjoy him. We're to laugh with him. God wants us to relish the life he's given us and praise him continually.

A young midwestern lawyer had a dark side to his nature in his early years. On one occasion his friends thought it wise to keep knives and razors out of his reach and to have someone stay with him through the night. During this period he wrote, "I am now the most miserable man living. If what I feel were equally distributed to the whole human family, there would not be one cheerful face on earth. Whether I shall ever be better I cannot tell; I awfully forebode I shall not. To remain as I am is impossible; I must die or be better, it appears to me."

Those words were written in 1841 by Abraham Lincoln. His law partner, William Hearndon, said that "melancholy dripped from him as he walked" during that time. But note how different he sounds in 1863: "The year that is drawing toward the close, has been filled with the blessings of fruitful fields and healthful skies. These bounties are so constantly enjoyed that we are prone to forget the source from which they come." He was painfully aware that thousands of America's young men were dying in the Civil War and that the country could be on the brink of collapse, but he was still able to see the goodness around him.

Sometime between 1841 and 1863, Lincoln had evidently learned certain habits of mind that enabled him to put much of his despairing tendency behind him. Not that he became carefree and blithely happy in those years when the republic shuddered; he would have been less a man had he suffered less. But he acquired an ability to live in the midst of tragedy and still cultivate qualities such as gratitude and joy. A clue to Lincoln's character may lie in a casual remark he once made to someone on the subject. "I've noticed," he said, "that most people are about as happy as they make up their minds to be."[1]

Lincoln made an important discovery. Thankfulness and praise are not attitudes that just happen. They are a conscious choice. Praise is not something dictated by circumstances. We decide whether or not we will praise God.

There's a second reason we are to praise God: *Praise focuses our minds on God.* The psalmist says, "I will extol the LORD at all times; his praise will always be on my lips" (Ps 34:1), and again, "It is good to praise the LORD and make music to your name, O Most High, to proclaim your love in the morning and your faithfulness at night" (Ps 92:1). Praise is good for us because it focuses our attention on God.

One of the most intriguing passages in all the Bible is found in 2 Chronicles 20. Jehoshaphat and the people of Judah are surrounded by a vast army, much greater in number than they. In the face of such odds, Jehoshaphat and the people turn to God in prayer. They praise God for his power and thank him for what he has done in the past. They tell God they have no hope except him. God responds to their worship by assuring them that they can trust him to take care of their enemies. Jehoshaphat demonstrates the importance of praise:

Early in the morning they left for the Desert of Tekoa. As they set out, Jehoshaphat stood and said, "Listen to me, Judah and people of Jerusalem! Have faith in the LORD your God and you will be upheld; have faith in his prophets and you will be successful." After consulting the people, Jehoshaphat appointed men to sing to the Lord and to praise him for the splendor of his holiness as they went out at the head of the army, saying:

"Give thanks to the LORD,

for his loves endures forever." (vv. 20-21)

What an unusual battle plan. He appoints the choir to go out before the army. Can you imagine being in the front row of the choir with enemies all around you? I'll bet you could hear a lot of cracking in the tenor section. How did praise help the people of Judah? It focused their minds on God and his greatness rather than on their scarcity of soldiers and weapons.

Some time ago I determined to set aside an afternoon to praise God. I realized that instead of thanking God for miracles he is performing and has already accomplished in our home and church, I am prone to focus my mind on things that still need to be done. There is nothing wrong with wanting to improve and achieve, but it causes ungratefulness when it keeps us from enjoying what God has already done. It becomes an obstacle to praise. So this particular afternoon, rather than laying problems and concerns before God and focusing on all the things that need attention in my family and in our church family, I decided I would simply praise God for who he is and thank him for what he's already done. I found that the more I focused on God and what he has already done, the more I gained a new sense of confidence for what he would do in the future.

It could be that you're facing difficult times right now. With all the things that have happened to you, you may feel like you can't praise God at the moment. Like Job, you're confused by what is happening in your life. You may even be questioning if God is watching out for you. In spite of the troubles you have encountered, I urge you to praise God. Thank him that you still have a relationship with God to sustain you. Tell him you'll praise him even when you don't understand. Focusing on God, his love and his power will make an amazing difference in your attitude.

That leads to a third reason we are to praise God: *Praise enables us to keep a proper perspective.* Praise reminds us how great God is and that he is more than a match for any problem we face. Psalm 135 declares,

Praise the LORD.

Praise the name of the LORD;

> praise him, you servants of the LORD. . . .

I know that the LORD is great,

> that our Lord is greater than all gods.

The LORD does whatever pleases him,

> in the heavens and on the earth,

> in the seas and all their depths. (vv. 1, 5)

Praise helps us remember that God is sovereign and fully in control. No situation catches him by surprise; there is nothing he cannot handle. Fixing our minds on God's power gives us a new perspective about whatever difficulties we may be facing.

Alan McGinnis, author of *The Friendship Factor,* was on a plane the night before Thanksgiving. He was sitting next to a jolly salesman. This man had been flying all day from upstate New York and had been stranded for the evening in Salt Lake City. Because of the delay he would not arrive home in Bakersfield, California, until 2 a.m. But was he irritable and tired like most of the travelers in the packed plane? No, he was happy, teasing two little children across the aisle, spreading good cheer to people.

"What do you sell?" Alan asked.

"Oil drilling tools."

"That's a tough business to be in these days, isn't it?"

"No," he replied. "It couldn't be better. We just opened another branch office this year, and it's doing great."

"But isn't the oil business in a terrible recession?"

"Yes, but we've decided not to participate," he said with a smile.

He went on to explain his company's success. "The industry slump has worked to our advantage because all our competitors are down in the mouth and complaining that they have to cut prices and can't make any money. That negative attitude rubs off on the customers. We, on the other hand, are not cutting our prices at all. But we're giving the best service of anybody in the industry, we're enthusiastic about our products, and we're very upbeat. Customers like doing business with sales people who have that attitude." He smiled again and said, "If this recession will just continue one more year, I'll make enough money to retire."[2]

Change your perspective and you can transform obstacles into opportunities. Even though it may appear that nothing is going right for you, you can determine to praise God anyway. And the very act of praise, out of obedience, can change your perspective and give you a deeper understanding of God's will for you.

One more reason we are called to praise is that *praise pushes back the spiritual forces of evil.* When Jehoshaphat and his people began to sing and praise God, "the LORD set ambushes against the men of Ammon and Moab and Mount Seir who were invading Judah, and they were defeated" (2 Chron 20:22). It was when they sang that God confused their enemies.

We find a similar release of God's power when Paul and Silas were thrown in prison for preaching Christ and delivering a young female slave from demon possession. "About midnight Paul and Silas were praying and singing hymns to God, and the other prisoners were listening to them. Suddenly there was such a violent earthquake that the foundations of the prison were shaken. At once all the prison doors flew open, and everybody's chains came loose" (Acts 16:25-26).

It was when they sang and praised God that he shook the prison and released the prisoners from their chains. Praise not only focuses our minds on God and changes our perspective, it releases the power of the Holy Spirit to push back the forces of evil.

Lloyd Ogilvie, former pastor of Hollywood Presbyterian Church, tells of an important decision he was facing that would affect the future of the church. It so happened that the decision locked him in a power struggle with an elder from the church who was outspokenly opposed to Ogilvie's plan. The conflict became a personal issue for both the officer and Ogilvie, and neither wanted to lose. If Ogilvie lost, it would cripple his future leadership; if the elder lost, he would lose face with people he had rallied to his cause.

Late one night, sleepless with concern over the situation, Ogilvie paced his bedroom floor. He was trying to convince God of how "right" he was and how dangerous this man was to the kingdom's growth in the church. "Simply praise me for this man and for the no-win situation you've gotten yourself into" was the only guidance he received. He spent the rest of the night doing that.

By morning he had a strange, mysterious feeling of release from the situation. What he had thought was the prelude to Armageddon was just one phase in God's strategy for the church. And to his surprise, he felt very differently about that church officer. For the first time in that long ordeal he asked, "I wonder where I missed with him? Why had I not followed my basic conviction of leadership that people can support only those things they share in developing?" Given his belief that a church can move no further or faster than the officers' ownership of the vision for the church, Ogilvie realized that he should pull back and include the man in the vision and, more than that, allow him to help shape the vision. After all, it was his church too! He felt an urge to call the elder. Yet Ogilvie feared that he would not respond and would see the call merely as the first stage of his victory in the conflict.

But someone else had been awake all that night too—the elder's wife. She had taken seriously a sermon Ogilvie had preached on praising the Lord as the key to unlocking difficulties. In response, she spent the night hours praising God for what they were all going through. That prompted her to follow the morning coffee she served her husband with a suggestion: "Why not call Lloyd, share your real feelings of not being consulted, and tell him you want what God wants, which may be better than what either of you think is his will?"

As a result of her commitment to praise the Lord, she had been given the gift of wisdom—and her husband was surprisingly responsive. He didn't know why, but he was open to her suggestion. She knew why!

As Ogilvie was putting off calling the man, the phone rang. A reserved but pleasant voice said, "I think we need to talk. Do you have an opening in your schedule today?" Did he! Ogilvie's positive response led to the first of many talks and a final decision that was a victory for neither man—but definitely a victory for the peace, unity and forward movement of the church. And praise had done it![3]

Is there someone in your church, school or workplace with whom you are having a struggle? Try praising God for this difficulty and for the person whom right now you may see as your enemy. God will give you a whole new love for the person and push back the forces of evil that thrive on discord.

Obstacles to Praise

C. S. Lewis in his book *Letters to Malcolm* identifies several obstacles to praise—things that keep us from adoring God.

The first is inattention. We get so busy with our many activities that we miss the overtures of divine love. The demands of home, family, school and work conspire to make life a blur. When we're breathlessly running on the treadmill of life, we overlook the little things God does. We cannot adore when we do not see.

Bob Edens was blind for fifty-one years. Couldn't see a thing. Life was a black tunnel of sounds, feelings, smells and tastes. Think of it—more than five decades of darkness. And then one day he could see! A skilled surgeon performed a new and complicated operation and, for the first time, Bob Edens had sight. He found it overwhelming.

I never would have dreamed that yellow is so . . . yellow. I don't have the words. I am amazed by yellow. But red is my favorite color. I just can't believe red. I can see the shape of the moon—and I like nothing better than seeing a jet plane flying across the sky, leaving a vapor trail. And of course, sunrises and sunsets.[4]

Edens is correct. We who have lived all our lives with sight cannot imagine being submerged in a world of darkness. But isn't it amazing? Though we have sight, we can be blind to the beauty that swarms all over us. Not just the yellows, purples, reds or greens, not just the vapor trails above us, but the flowers below us and the incredible displays of art around us. I have in mind the innumerable blessings that come to us. How easy to spend our days blind to the benefits that we take for granted.

The second obstacle to praise is misguided attention. When frustrations occur, all we are aware of is trouble. We focus on problems and ignore the fragrance of deity. When you say, "Beautiful day today, isn't it?" misguided attention responds, "First nice day we've had all year" or "Oh, it's too hot; I wish it were cooler."

Every year I read through the Bible. When I come to the book of Exodus each year, I never cease to be amazed at how quickly the people of Israel forgot God's mighty miracles in bringing them out of Egypt. Instead, they complained that Moses brought them out to the desert to die by the hand of Pharaoh's army or to die of thirst or starvation. Their attention was misguided. They focused on the negative instead of the positive, on the impossible instead of the possible.

A third obstacle to praise is greed. Instead of thanking God for his gifts, we may say the fatal word "Encore." When we ask for an encore, we may be asking for more than God is pleased to give. Instead of simply enjoying what God has given, we demand more. We're never satisfied. So we never enjoy God and his bounties.

Some psychologists tried an experiment with children. A group of preschool children were placed in a room where they could be observed through a one-way window. The room was stocked with all kinds of toys. But these weren't just any toys. They were all broken. There was a telephone without a receiver, a doll without an arm, cars without the wheels, tables without chairs and so forth. The children played happily all morning long.

The next morning the children were placed in the same room with the dilapidated old toys. This time, however, a curtain was drawn, revealing a window that showed them another room full of toys. Through the window, the children saw all kinds of perfect toys: a telephone with a receiver, dolls with all their body parts, cars fully intact, tables with chairs and so on. As we might expect, on the second morning the fun stopped. The children no longer played with their broken toys. Instead, most stood at the window crying for the good toys.

What happened? Once their expectations were raised, they became unhappy with their lot. Their focus changed from what they had to what they didn't have. If you allow your mind to dwell on the things you do not have, you'll never be happy. If you want to take out the root of complaining and bitterness, pull the weeds of expectations.

Steppingstones to Praise

Thanksgiving and praise are seldom the first words on our lips. We need all the help we can get in order to move into a fuller adoration of God. I find that most people don't want to be negative thinkers who complain. They simply don't know how to overcome their circumstances through praise. We need to be coached if we are to become praisers. The following steppingstones will, I hope, help mark the way.

Steppingstone one instructs us to pay attention to little things. If an obstacle to praise is inattention, a corrective is to pay attention. Stop and notice the flower blooming by your doorstep, the wind rustling through the leaves, the little creatures that creep across your driveway. Don't try to analyze them. Just watch the birds and the squirrels and the ducks. Take a moment to feel the grass beneath your bare feet. Notice the little things that are ours to enjoy.

Dietrich Bonhoeffer in his classic *Life Together* writes, "Only he who gives thanks for the little things receives the big things. How can God entrust great things to one who will not thankfully receive from him the little things?"[5] Make a game out of it today. See how many little things you can notice that God has given you to enjoy.

Steppingstone two asks us to practice gratitude. We can now develop a habit of giving thanks for the simple gifts that come our way. Start by giving thanks for little things. The psalmist writes, "Give thanks to the LORD, for he is good" (Ps 136:1). Practice whispering prayers of thanks to God hundreds of times each day. Thanks draw us beyond the tiny pleasures to the Giver of pleasures. Balance every complaint with ten gratitudes, each criticism with ten compliments. When we practice gratitude, the time will come when we find our prayers not filled so much with "please" as with "thank you."

Start by giving thanks for the small things, then gradually cultivate an attitude of giving thanks in all situations. Then we may be better able to understand what Paul means in 1 Thessalonians 5:18: "In everything give thanks, for this is God's will for you in Christ Jesus" (NASB). Some people have misunderstood this verse to mean that we should give thanks *for* all things. This would inevitably lead us to give thanks for evil. The Greek text tells us not to give thanks *for* all things but *in* every situation. For example, if you are robbed, you don't need to thank God for the robbery, but you might thank God that although the robber took your possessions, he did not take your life. You might thank God that although the robber took valuable property, things can be replaced. If you learn to thank God even in difficult circumstances, you can turn every calamity into a blessing.

Thomas Edison serves as an example of a robust personality who never caved in to disaster. He knew how to turn adversity into advantage. In 1914 the great Edison laboratories in New Jersey were almost entirely destroyed by fire. In one night Edison lost $2 million worth of equipment and the record of much of his life's work.

The next morning, walking about the charred embers of so many of his hopes and dreams, the sixty-seven-year-old Edison said, "There is great value in disaster. All our mistakes are burned up. Thank God we can start anew."

Rather than brooding over his losses, Edison focused on something positive that he found in the tragedy. He was a true inventor who had learned not to focus on failed experiments. Gratitude in all situations takes our focus off ourselves and our problems and turns our gaze toward God, where it belongs.

Steppingstone three admonishes us to exalt God. David writes, "Glorify the LORD with me; let us exalt his name together" (Ps 34:3). To exalt God means to lift him up high. It means to magnify God. To magnify ourselves or our problems out of proportion is dangerous, but when we magnify God we are on safe ground. We cannot exaggerate his greatness beyond what is actually the case. Reading and memorizing the psalms is of great assistance here. Music is of great help as well. It can ease even sad hearts into adoration. At home, in the car or wherever we are, we can sing praises to God.

Steppingstone four reminds us to celebrate God. Celebration is best done in community. We come together to joyously celebrate who God is and all he has done for us. When Christians gather to worship, the main event is the celebration of God.

The key to celebrating God is the heart. Without the heart there is no worship; it is mere stage play, simply acting out a part. There's no passion, no feeling. We are hypocrites. We cannot be said to be worshiping God if we lack sincerity of heart. An attitude of praise and thanksgiving is God's will for us, it keeps our minds focused on God rather than on our problems, it pushes back the spiritual forces of evil, and it gives us a whole new perspective in the face of the obstacles and troubles we encounter. When you worship this week, see that it is heartfelt. It will transform your worship.

The Last Word

Our five-year-old son has been diagnosed with attention deficit disorder and acute hyperactivity. He is in constant motion. When he has not taken his medicine or has eaten something sweet, he runs around as if he had ants in his pants. Jorie and I have had our hands full with him from the day he was born. We have to keep our eye on him all the time. Since we do not let Mark eat much of anything that contains sugar, one of his favorite stratagems is to get up early, slip down to the kitchen and help himself to a gourmet breakfast without anyone monitoring his intake.

Every year in July and August our family looks forward to picking a huge crop of blackberries in our backyard. Last fall Jorie used some of them to bake a large, delicious pie. Our family of eight devoured about three-fourths of it after supper that evening, and Jorie then announced that the last two pieces would be for Mom and Dad.

All through the following day I looked forward to that piece of pie. After dinner I went to cut the pie, only to discover that it was gone. I found the empty pie pan stuffed under the couch in the family room—Mark's favorite eating hideout. I turned to him and asked, "Did you eat the pie?"

Very slowly he began nodding his head with that *I'm-in-deep-trouble* look. I learned that Mark had polished off our pie at the crack of dawn, before the rest of us were awake.

One of Mark's crowning efforts, however, took place in the bathroom. Having found a razor blade in the tub, he worked quietly by himself for quite a while, then emerged with shockingly large bald spots all over his head. Jorie and I were really unhappy with him, to say the least.

Later that day I took him along as I did errands. In the grocery store the checkout clerk said, "Ah, he's been playing with scissors, I see."

"Razor," I corrected her.

"You know why God made him so cute?" she replied. "To keep him alive."

I chuckled to myself as I loaded the groceries into the car. *There's a lady who knows what she's talking about.* Sometimes kids do things that make you feel like strangling them. So God must make naughty kids particularly cute to help them survive.

That afternoon I determined that rather than being disgusted with Mark for the naughty things he does, I would praise God for him. I praised God that he cut only his hair and not his scalp. I praised God for bringing this endless bundle of energy into our home. I thanked the Lord that Mark had invited Christ into his heart. I told Christ how grateful I was for Mark's pleasant disposition. He is the happiest member of the Kincaid tribe. No one laughs or smiles more than he.

My decision to praise God gave me a whole new perspective. I found myself playing with Mark and loving him more, and by the end of the day he was more obedient. Praise made the difference.

How are you doing at praising and thanking God? Maybe a lack of gratitude may explain why God's will seems a little murky to you. Possibly it seems pointless to God to guide you further into the knowledge of his will when you have not obeyed his request for you to become a praiser. Try praising God right now.

Questions for Reflection and Discussion

1. Read 2 Chronicles 20:22. Do you think praise subdues the spiritual forces of evil? Why or why not?

2. Read Psalm 113:1-3. Why does God command us to praise him? How can praise be genuine if it comes in response to a command?

3. Read Psalm 95:1-2. How does praise help us to keep our problems in perspective?

4. Why does God want us to thank him for little things?

How do you feel you fail to praise God for little things due to inattention?

5. Do you feel you truly exalt and celebrate God when you go to church to worship? Why or why not?

6. What principle or insight in this chapter was most helpful to you?

EIGHT

The Necessity of Confession in Obtaining Guidance

◆

SOME time ago the *Chicago Tribune* offered readers a chance to make public confessions of things that were bothering them. The editors suspected that people suffered from things that weighed heavily on their conscience. What they did not anticipate was the volume of people who would respond and the types of things they would reveal.

One woman confessed that during the four months she was trapped in the same house with her husband during their divorce proceedings, she cleaned all three toilets with a washcloth, which she dutifully hung by her husband's clean towel.

Another admitted to putting fishing worms on a friend's hamburger. She reported that she came into the kitchen one day with an armload of sweet corn and screamed in panic when she saw a spider on her body. George, the host, ignored her screams. (He claimed later that he had not seen the spider; if he had, he would have brushed it off.) She didn't believe him and to test his eyesight put five fishing worms on an open-face hamburger, which George proceeded to eat, apparently without seeing the worms. She said she had not intended to let him eat the worms, but an unrelated family crisis distracted her.

Many of us carry memories that weigh on our conscience. We need to confess these wrongs to God. The first step in a relationship with God is to honestly admit our sin against him.

How important is confession in obtaining guidance? It is absolutely essential. The psalmist tells us, "If I had cherished sin in my heart, the Lord would not have listened" (Ps 66:18). If there is sin in my life that I have not confessed or am unwilling to relinquish, then my prayers go unheeded. It is not that God refuses to answer our prayers when we are rebelling against him. God always listens when we pray. It is, rather, that when we are living in sin we do not pray. We don't want to pray. It's the last thing we want to do. We feel too unworthy to expect God to answer. We reason that, since we are not doing what God wants, why should he do what we want?

Why Confession Is Necessary

We don't obtain guidance from God not so much because God is unwilling to give it but because we sense we don't deserve to receive it. So unless we confess our sins and come clean with God, we cannot hope to obtain guidance. I find in Scripture at least three reasons confession is a necessity to obtaining guidance.

First, it is a prerequisite for forgiveness. Jesus says in the Lord's Prayer, " 'Forgive us our debts, as we also have forgiven our debtors.'. . . For if you forgive men when they sin against you, your heavenly Father will also forgive you. But if you do not forgive men their sins, your Father will not forgive your sins" (Mt 6:12, 14). We sometimes interpret this teaching as a kind of cosmic tit for tat. "You forgive others," we imagine God saying, "then I'll forgive you. Otherwise, no dice."

Surely we know God better than that. To think of this as a kind of "quid pro quo" prayer—if we forgive those who wrong us, then forgiveness is our due—is, of course, to completely misunderstand it. Rather, Jesus lays down a principle: If we refuse to forgive, we so harden our hearts that God's forgiveness cannot reach us. We grow an impenetrable callus of the soul. If we are unwilling to forgive, it is not that God refuses to forgive us but that we make ourselves unforgivable. God's grace is still there for us, but it cannot reach us because our hearts are hardened, so we do not come to God for mercy.

What do you gain from prayer? How do you feel after you worship God? When you go to church to worship, do you return a changed person? Or do you feel like you have not really met with God but have only been going through the motions? We can worship God only with sincerity of heart. Confession enables us to begin a relationship with God by approaching him in honesty.

Second, confession is a prerequisite for confidence in prayer. As we saw earlier, the psalmist writes, "If I had cherished sin in my heart, the Lord would not have listened" (Ps 66:18). When we do not confess our sins, we have no assurance that our prayers will be answered. James says, "The prayer of a righteous man is powerful and effective" (Jas 5:16). What kind of prayers for guidance are effective? The prayers of righteous people. If we want to grow in the knowledge of God's will, we must approach God with confession.

In John 15:7 Jesus says, "If you remain in me and my words remain in you, ask whatever you wish, and it will be given you." What a promise! Ask whatever you want, and it will be done for you. But there's a condition. You must remain in him. You must obey. Christ says that God will take you seriously, if you take him seriously. He'll do what you ask, if you do what he asks.

John says much the same in 1 John 3:22: We "receive from him anything we ask, because we obey his commands and do what pleases him." Confession of sin and obedience are essential to obtaining guidance in prayer.

Third, confession is a prerequisite for victory over Satan. Paul writes, "'In your anger do not sin': Do not let the sun go down while you are still angry, and do not give the devil a foothold" (Eph 4:26-27). When we don't get rid of anger but hold on to bitterness or resentment, we give Satan a foothold. When we do not confess and get rid of our sin, we give the devil an opportunity to defeat us.

Paul says the same in 2 Corinthians 2:5-11: "If anyone has caused grief . . . you ought to forgive . . . in order that Satan might not outwit us. For we are not unaware of his schemes." Satan's scheme is to entice Christians into disharmony in relationships and to lure them into thinking that it's not important to forgive those who have injured them. Don't succumb to such thinking. Unconfessed sin and bitterness leave us under Satan's power.

We saw in chapter seven that prayer is a means of invading and conquering enemy territory. Confessing sin or admitting bitterness toward someone may be the weapon you need to gain victory over the spiritual forces of evil. Is there someone you are unwilling to forgive? Someone who took advantage of you or hurt you deeply? A parent? A child? A spouse? A business associate? A teacher? Unless I miss my guess, there is probably someone you really don't want to forgive. I beg you, don't withhold your forgiveness. It's essential to gaining victory over Satan. Triumph over your enemy is essential if you are to grow in your understanding of God's will.

Elements in the Process of Confession

You ask, "How do I confess my sins and show I am truly sorry for my sin?" Let me suggest six elements in the process of confession.

Element number one is personal confession. This entails confessing to God the ways we have sinned against him. Nehemiah writes,

> While I was in the citadel of Susa, Hanani, one of my brothers, came from Judah with some other men, and I questioned them about the Jewish remnant that survived the exile, and also about Jerusalem. They said to me, "Those who survived the exile and are back in the province are in great trouble and disgrace. The wall of Jerusalem is broken down, and its gates have been burned with fire." (Neh 1:1-3)

Nehemiah, still in captivity, questioned some Jews who had returned from Judah as to how the remnant was doing in Jerusalem. He learned that the city lay in ruins because the wall had not been rebuilt. This was a disgrace. The walls were not just a physical problem; they represented a theological tragedy. The Jews were God's representatives to the world. When their city was in disrepair, it was a reproach to God's name.

After receiving this tragic report, Nehemiah took his concerns to God in prayer:

When I heard these things, I sat down and wept. For some days I mourned and fasted and prayed before the God of heaven. Then I said: "O LORD, God of heaven, the great and awesome God, who keeps his covenant of love with those who love him and obey his commands, let your ear be attentive and your eyes open to hear the prayer your servant is praying before you day and night for your servants, the people of Israel. I confess the sins we Israelites, including myself and my father's house, have committed against you." (Neh 1:4-6)

He began his prayer by confessing his own sins. He admitted that he was part of the problem.

When we face a problem, we like to think that other people have caused it. We don't like to admit that we may have helped. We say things such as "I can make it up" or "I will give it back" or "I'll apologize" or "I wasn't myself when I did that" or "No one knows about it" or "But I'm going to quit" or "It's a dangerous habit" or "What's done can't be undone." All nice excuses used as a means of rationalizing our culpability.

Lloyd H. Steffen tells of a time when King Frederick II, an eighteenth-century king of Prussia, was visiting a prison in Berlin. The inmates tried to prove to him how they had been unjustly imprisoned. All except one. He sat quietly in a corner, while all the rest protested their innocence. Seeing him sitting there oblivious to the commotion, the king asked him what he was imprisoned for. "Armed robbery, Your Honor."

The king asked, "Were you guilty?"

"Yes Sir," he answered. "I entirely deserve my punishment."

The king then gave an order to the guard: "Release this guilty man. I don't want this guilty man corrupting all these other innocent inmates."[1]

Isn't that like us? We're quick to blame others for our troubles, but slow to admit our own mistakes. But if we are to come clean with God, we must first confess our own sins.

We need to be honest with God if we want to come into his presence, and when we do, we feel better about ourselves.

A young woman came to me for counsel. She told me about her

problems. Then she said, "It feels like I'm confessing to a priest . . . but it feels good." James writes, "Confess your sins to each other and pray for each other so that you may be healed" (Jas 5:16).

We like to think that the only person to whom we need to tell our sins is Christ, but when we admit our sins to others, we are far more likely to experience the pardoning grace of God. Why is this? James knows that when we confess to another human being there is a greater likelihood that we are serious about our confession. Furthermore, our friend can hold us accountable for our repentance.

Element number two is corporate confession. Nehemiah confessed not only his own sin but also the sins of all the people of Israel. He lamented, "We have acted very wickedly toward you. We have not obeyed the commands" (Neh 1:7). He prayed on behalf of all God's people.

Karl Barth went back to Germany after World War II. Theologian after theologian came up to him and groaned, "We have been through a demonic period with Adolf Hitler." Even non-Christians were saying, "What we've experienced was demonic." Everyone claimed, in effect, "The devil was responsible." Barth said he yearned to hear someone say, "We sinned." He felt they wouldn't get help until they admitted their own culpability. Churches today yearn for pastors who are transparent, leaders willing to admit their mistakes, shepherds who admit their sins, ministers who identify with the people.

Two years ago, our pastoral staff attended a prayer summit with 175 other pastors from the Pacific Northwest. We spent three days together with no agenda other than prayer. The first day we spent praising God. The second day we focused on confession. As we gathered in small groups, pastors began to confess prayerlessness. They admitted feelings of bitterness toward other ministries in their area. Several ministers acknowledged anger toward elders or parishioners within their church, or bitterness against God because their churches had not grown. A number confessed addictions to pornography. Some pastors broke down and wept unashamedly.

Months after the summit, I continued to receive reports of great things God was doing in the churches represented at the gathering. Barriers had been broken down between pastors and churches. Worship attendance increased dramatically in several churches. I believe that much of the fruit born out of that experience can be attributed to the confession and repentance that occurred among pastors.

We have a tendency to blame others for deadness in the church and immorality in our country. We don't like to admit we're part of the church and country. Until we admit our guilt in allowing or causing our church and country to become what they are, we will never know God's healing. God says, "If my people, who are called by my name, will humble themselves and pray and seek my face and turn from their wicked ways, then will I hear from heaven and will forgive their sin and will heal their land" (2 Chron 7:14). We must admit our corporate solidarity with the church and the nation and plead for God's mercy.

Element number three is tears. Most Christians underestimate the value of tears in confession. But men and women who march across the pages of Scripture were well-acquainted with the grace of tears. Nehemiah tells us that he wept for days (Neh 1:4). Job declares, "My eye pours out tears to God" (Job 16:20). Almost every page of the Psalter is wet with the tears of the singers. "I am worn out from groaning," laments David; "all night long I flood my bed with weeping and drench my couch with tears" (Ps 6:6). The singer who so beautifully describes our soul's thirst for God as a deer longing for streams of water goes on to confess, "My tears have been my food day and night" (Ps 42:3).

You say, "What is all this about weeping and mourning? It sounds depressing. Is this a throwback to the days of false guilt and unhealthy repressions? Aren't we to be happy?" Yes, God wants us to be joyful, but the path to happiness is reached only by passing through the river of confession and tears.

When was the last time you were so grieved over your sin or concerned about some person, issue or problem that you wept? Don't let yourself get away with the "I'm just not the emotional type" excuse. We've learned to approach God with our minds, rather than with our tears. We need to get in touch with our emotive center when we pray. Tears are a symbol of genuine confession. Sometimes God cannot lead us into a deeper experience of his will because we have not wept for the ways we have transgressed God's commands.

A fourth element that is essential to confession is reconciliation with those we injure. It is not enough to simply ask God to forgive us and admit our guilt to others. We must go to these people and make amends.

Moses gave the law of restitution: "When a man or woman wrongs another in any way and so is unfaithful to the LORD, that person is guilty and must confess the sin he has committed. He must make full restitution for his wrong, add one fifth to it and give it all to the person he has wronged" (Num 5:5-7). Confession plus restitution provide the basis for reconciliation.

In Matthew 5:23 Jesus says, "Therefore, if you are offering your gift at the altar and there remember that your brother has something against you, leave your gift there in front of the altar. First go and be reconciled to your brother; then come and offer your gift." Failure to reconcile with your neighbor negatively impacts your ability to worship. When God brings to mind someone you have hurt, you are to stop your prayer and go make peace with that person. Then you can continue your worship.

When Jorie's first husband died of cancer at twenty-four years of age, her in-laws were quite cruel to her. By their actions and attitudes they communicated complete rejection of Jorie. His parents owned an insurance policy on their son. They kept all the money and made no effort to help Jorie with her thousands and thousands of dollars of medical and funeral expenses. Jorie felt bitterness toward them, and rightfully so, for they treated her with gross insensitivity. Resentment welled up within her . . . until several years later.

Jorie was teaching a class in which she was focusing on the importance of forgiveness. As she prepared, she realized she had some unfinished business in her life. She decided that even though her former in-laws had been extremely unfair to her, she did not have a completely clear conscience toward them. She wrote them a letter asking them to forgive her for her bitterness and failure to fully understand the hurt and pain they must have felt in losing their prized and oldest son to cancer. A few weeks later she received a letter from them in which they offered their forgiveness and expressed great thankfulness for her letter.

Jorie needn't have taken that step. They were more in the wrong than she. But she wanted a completely clear conscience so that she could experience the freedom that comes from knowing she could look them in the eye with a clear conscience. She recognized that she could not expect to grow deeper in the knowledge of God's will if she allowed resentment, an attitude that is clearly outside God's will, to take up residence in her life.

Element number five is repentance. Genuine biblical confession always includes repentance. To repent means to turn from sin. It requires a plan of action so that we do not repeat the same transgression over and over. Proverbs 28:13 tells us, "He who conceals his sins does not prosper, but whoever confesses and renounces them finds mercy." We must confess and renounce our sins.

Numerous times after I have hurt Jorie, I have come to her, said I was sorry and asked her to forgive me. Numerous times her answer has been no. "What's the matter?" I ask her. "Do you have a problem with lack of forgiveness?"

"No," she replies. "You don't think you're wrong."

Although I don't like it when I receive this kind of response, I have to admit that she makes a good point. She can tell by my attitude or tone of voice that I really don't believe I was wrong.

Other times when I have asked her to forgive me, even when I have admitted my guilt, I've encountered the same negative reply. This time she adds, "You're just going to do it again. Why should I forgive you? You never change."

Once again, I must admit she's right. I really don't have a plan in place to change. She has seen me do certain things over and over again. Confession without repentance is always hollow.

A sixth element of confession that I believe is far more important than many people realize is fasting. Somehow most believers have come to the conclusion that fasting has gone out of style. But it is impossible to overlook the fact that many of the most impassioned prayers in the Bible were accompanied by fasting. Moses fasted and prayed before the Lord forty days and forty nights because of all the sins of the people of Israel. Obviously, fasting was of high value to Moses.

Then once again I fell prostrate before the LORD for forty days and forty nights; I ate no bread and drank no water, because of all the sin you had committed, doing what was evil in the LORD's sight and so provoking him to anger. I feared the anger and wrath of the Lord, for he was angry enough with you to destroy you. But again the LORD listened to me. (Deut 9:18-19)

Fasting created the atmosphere Moses needed to pray a powerful prayer.

Ezra fasted and prayed that God would grant his people safe passage to Jerusalem (Ezra 8:21). When Nehemiah heard that the walls of Jerusalem were torn down and the city lay in ruins, he mourned and fasted and prayed for days before attempting to rebuild the wall (Neh 1:4).

When Daniel cried out for God to restore the people of Israel to Jerusalem, he "pleaded with [God] in prayer and petition, in fasting, and in sackcloth and ashes" (Dan 9:3). Another time he fasted and prayed for three weeks before receiving a vision from God (Dan 10:2-3).

The people of Nineveh neither ate nor drank as a symbol of their repentance. As a result, God had compassion and did not bring the destruction on them Jonah had prophesied (Jon 3:5, 10).

You say, "These are from the Old Testament. What about the New Testament?" Jesus fasted for forty days in the wilderness (Mt 4:2). If he needed to fast, how much more must we? He also instructed us to fast. In Matthew 6:16 Jesus said, "When you fast"—he assumed that we would fast. In Matthew 9:15 Jesus declared, "The time will come when the bridegroom will be taken from them; then they will fast." Jesus taught that after he ascended to heaven, his disciples would fast. In Acts 13:3 the church fasted and prayed before sending Barnabas and Saul on their missionary journey.

How does fasting help us obtain guidance? It increases our power in prayer and heightens our spiritual antennae so that we can perceive God's will. Am I suggesting that we earn God's favor by starving ourselves to death? Is this some throwback to the theology of medieval asceticism?

We don't have to impress God and beg him to give us what we need. We saw in chapter five from the parable of the friend at midnight that God is a loving Father who waits for you to call and longs to meet your needs. But fasting is a means of signaling to God and ourselves that we really mean business in our prayers. For most of us, giving up cherished meals is a big sacrifice. No sacrifice we make for God's kingdom goes unnoticed by the Father. Jesus says in Matthew 6:16 that when you fast, you should do it in secret, "and your Father, who sees what is done in secret, will reward you."

Fasting also enables us to have heightened spiritual sensitivity. It is an outward expression of inner repentance and godly sorrow. This spiritual mourning enables us to subdue sin and be more alert to God's leading. When I fast, I find that my mind is keener, and I'm able to focus longer in prayer. Fasting has enabled me to be more aware of Christ's direction for my life and has preceded some of my greatest spiritual victories.

A word about some of the mechanics of fasting. What exactly do I mean by the term *fasting?* Some people use the term to describe a period a time when they give up a particular activity, much as some people do during Lent. Some people go without both food and water when they fast. Most often, it refers to a period of time when we just go without food. In fact, drinking water is highly recommended.

In most of the Scriptures we've examined, one man paid the price by fasting and intercession, and an entire nation was delivered from judgment. Do we even dare guess what might take place in our homes and schools and churches if Christians awoke to their right and responsibility to wield such power through prayer and fasting? Can you envision the unending procession of liberated lives streaming out of darkness into the kingdom of light? Can you hear the happy cries of mothers and fathers saturating the heavens as wayward sons and daughters come to Jesus? Can you see Satan cower in defeat as hundreds of intercessors invade his citadel and set free the captives of sin? Can you imagine how much clearer God's will might be to us if we made it a practice to fast and pray regularly?

When was the last time you fasted to break the power of sin in your life? When was the last occasion that you fasted and interceded on behalf of your marriage, your children, your friends, your church, your country? How long has it been since you fasted so that you might better ascertain God's will for you?

The Last Word

Confession is absolutely essential to obtaining guidance in prayer. When we pray or worship, the essential starting point is to be honest with God and admit who we are. Confession enables us to see how far short we fall in keeping God's commandments. Confession is a humbling experience, but it provides us with a transforming catharsis.

Dick Halverson, former chaplain of the U.S. Senate, was serving Communion in his church one Sunday. As he passed the plate to an elder, the church leader declined. The next day Dick went to see him and said, "Frank, I am troubled that you didn't take Communion the other day."

The elder responded, "I just didn't feel worthy."

Dick replied, "If you ever feel worthy, then don't take Communion. It is your unworthiness that qualifies you to take Communion."

We are all unworthy of Christ's love and forgiveness. Only as we admit this truth are we prepared to partake of Holy Communion. When we confess our sins, we put ourselves in a position to hear and understand God's will.

Questions for Reflection and Discussion

1. Why is confession a prerequisite for confidence in our prayers?

2. Read Nehemiah 1:7 and Daniel 9:7-14. What is the significance of these godly leaders' identifying with the people and sharing in their guilt?

Do you feel that most pastors and Christian leaders share in the responsibility for our churches' and nation's sin? Why or why not?

3. Why are tears important in the process of confession?

Describe a time you wept for your sins.

4. Read Proverbs 28:13. Why is repentance an essential element in confession?

5. Why is fasting important to the process of ascertaining God's will?

What part does fasting play in your life?

6. What principle or insight in this chapter was most significant to you?

NINE

Praying for God's Will in Healing

◆

MUTEMI Mwinzi was a very sick man. A member of a church in Kenya, in 1963 he was stricken by a strange illness that none of the doctors seemed able to treat or relieve. Though he prayed, took medication and even consulted a witch doctor, he resigned himself to the sad truth that he probably would soon die. Once he had been diagnosed with a terminal illness, people abandoned him. Family and friends refused to care for him. They came by each day to see him, but not because they cared. They only stopped by to see if he had died.

Mutemi, who knew a few verses in the Bible, remembered Psalm 27:10: "My father and my mother have forsaken me, but the Lord will take me up" (NASB). He quoted the verse over and over and cried out repeatedly to God for help. When he realized there was no more hope, he dragged himself outside to die. About ten yards from his hut, he pleaded with God one more time to either heal him or let him die. He promised the Lord that if he was healed, he would spend the rest of his life serving him and would give all that he had to the church.

As he whispered his resolve to the Lord, his body began to shiver. Within moments he crumpled to the ground in convulsions. He drifted into unconsciousness. When he awakened, the sickness was gone—completely. For the first time in days he felt hungry. He walked back into his small house to find something to eat. Some time later, when his family and friends found him eating at the table, he explained to them everything that had happened.

The following Sunday, Mutemi told his story to a church filled with people. Many of those who had never been in church before went forward to receive Christ. The church experienced instant revival. Mutemi, who was a wealthy man by village standards, promised to take responsibility for the pastor's salary and to build a new church. Men and women came from around the country to hear his story. Within a year, the church membership grew from fifty to three hundred people.[1] The sudden growth came as a result of the healing power of the Holy Spirit.

A Christian woman in the United States had been given only a few weeks to live. Cancer filled her body. Her doctors informed her that there was nothing more that they could do for her. She had given up hope. Then she was invited to see the movie *Jesus,* the story of the life of Christ based on the Gospel of Luke. This film, produced by Campus Crusade for Christ, has been translated into dozens of languages and seen by hundreds of thousands of people around the world.

As the cancer victim sat through the showing, Jesus Christ came alive to her as never before. She realized that he was the God of the living, who healed the sick and the lame. She had a sudden realization that the Christ she observed on the screen not only healed people when he walked this earth but was still alive and able to heal her that very day. Sitting in the darkened theater, she believed God for her complete healing.

She went to her scheduled appointment for more medical tests the next day. As her doctor examined her, he was dumbfounded by the results. He hastily requested a new battery of tests. To his utter amazement, not one test showed a trace of the cancer that had filled her body just the week before. Christ had miraculously healed her.[2]

When my wife, Jorie, was a junior at Wheaton College, she married the star of the soccer team, a two-year All-American forward. Her husband, Paul, enrolled at Trinity Evangelical Divinity School to prepare to become a pastor. Four months after their wedding, Paul was diagnosed with cancer of the spinal cord. Instead of enjoying honeymoon living, the newlyweds encountered a barrage of medical tests, surgeries, chemotherapy and pain medications.

Throughout his painful eighteen-month decline, he and Jorie prayed for God to heal him. Since he had committed his life to serving the Lord and had a lifetime of ministry before him, they believed God would heal him. Godly professors from Wheaton College and Trinity Seminary anointed him with oil and prayed for healing. Thousands of people in the Chicago area and around the country lifted up prayers on his behalf. Nevertheless, after nearly two years of battling with his illness, Paul's life drew to a close.

Two people healed; one not. All three trusted in Christ; two were made well, one died. How are we to develop a doctrine of healing from such divergent experiences? What is God's will for his people in this matter of healing? Unfortunately, most Christians move to one of two extremes.

At one pole are those who claim that God no longer heals today. They neither expect nor pray for miracles of healing. They hold no healing services. The tragic result? People suffer needlessly because they never ask God to heal. At the other pole Christians pursue healing with such zeal that it becomes the primary focus of their faith. They expect God to heal every sniffle or scratch. They report marvelous accounts of healing. One person said, "Those excited about the healing work of the Holy Spirit tell the truth, the whole truth, and a little more than the truth." In other words, they tend to exaggerate. They tell of healings but skip the nonhealings. People not healed are rebuked for lack of faith.

What are we to believe in this matter of healing? Is it always God's will that his people be healed of sickness? Is it always God's desire that we pray for healing? On the other hand, can we expect too much from God in the realm of healing and fall into disillusionment? If we do not experience God's healing power in our lives, is it because we are faithless and refuse to appropriate the healing power God offers us? Or is it because we have replaced faith in God with confidence in modern medicine?

Everyone agrees that the Old Testament prophets, Jesus and New Testament apostles healed people. A quick survey of Christians today reveals that God is still in the business of healing. Almost no one doubts that God can still heal today. But how are we to interpret the fact that many people who pray for healing are not healed? We not only need a theology of healing, we need a theology of nonhealing as well. We come a long way toward solving this enigma when we understand the different ways God heals.

Intervention

One way God heals is through what we might call an intervention. God reaches down and removes the illness, usually instantaneously. He supernaturally intervenes in history. Interventions are what we find in Jesus' miracles. He healed so powerfully that most people watched with mouths wide open, utterly astonished.

Mark's Gospel records what most people believe to be Peter's sermons. Read Peter's eyewitness account of Jesus healing the daughter of an important synagogue official: "Then one of the synagogue rulers, named Jairus, came there. Seeing Jesus, he fell at his feet and pleaded earnestly with him, 'My little daughter is dying. Please come and put your hands on her so that she will be healed and live.' So Jesus went with him" (Mk 5:22-24).

As Jesus followed the Jewish leader, the procession was interrupted by a woman who reached out to touch Jesus' garment. The moment she touched his robe, she felt his healing power instantly cure her ailing body—a divine intervention. Jesus stopped and assured the woman that her faith had made her well.

The delay must have driven Jairus crazy, who knew that every minute was critical for his dying daughter. Mark continues his account: "While Jesus was still speaking, some men came from the house of Jairus, the synagogue ruler. 'Your daughter is dead,' they said. 'Why bother the teacher any more?' " (Mk 5:35). There's only one message more foreboding than "Your daughter is going to die," and that is "Your daughter is dead." It is final.

"Ignoring what they said, Jesus told the synagogue ruler, 'Don't be afraid; just believe.' He did not let anyone follow him except Peter, James and John the brother of James" (Mk 5:36-37). Jesus took only three disciples along. We love to sensationalize. We would want as many people as possible to see. Not Jesus. He took three.

> When they came to the home of the synagogue ruler, Jesus saw a commotion, with people crying and wailing loudly. He went in and said to them, "Why all this commotion and wailing? The child is not dead but asleep." But they laughed at him.
>
> After he put them all out, he took the child's father and mother and the disciples who were with him, and went in where the child was. He took her by the hand and said to her, *"Talitha koum!"* (which means, "Little girl, I say to you, get up!"). Immediately the girl stood up and walked around. . . . At this they were completely astonished. (Mk 5:38-42)

The girl was healed immediately and completely. It was an intervention of God. James, the leader of the Jewish Christian church in Jerusalem, teaches us about God's same healing power still available to the church.

> Is any one of you in trouble? He should pray. Is anyone happy? Let him sing songs of praise. Is any one of you sick? He should call the elders of the church to pray over him and anoint him with oil in the name of the Lord. And the prayer offered in faith will make the sick person well; the Lord will raise him up. (Jas 5:13-15)

James tells us that when we are sick we are to come to the pastors and the ruling elders in the church. We should ask them to anoint us with oil and pray that we be healed. The oil is not used as a medicine but as part of the healing prayer. For centuries the church used anointing as a means of healing the sick. In fact, the sacrament of unction, or anointing, was, in the early centuries, designed as a means of cure, not as a preparation for death as it now is in the Roman Catholic Church. It was not until A.D. 852 that the sacrament became Extreme Unction, to prepare a person for death. We need to restore and elevate the practice of elders praying for the sick in the church.

James goes on to tell us that prayer offered in faith makes the sick person well. When petitions for healing are made in faith, it brings results. The faith lies in the elders, not in the sick person (about whose faith nothing is said). It is the elders' faith that is critical: if something "goes wrong," it is they, not the sick person, who bear the responsibility. This means that the church cannot deploy elders who think prayer for healing is hocus-pocus. They must firmly believe that it is God's will to heal people today.

Furthermore, James promises us, when we follow this prescribed practice for healing in the church, God will raise up the sick person. James is quite clear about the source of the healing. It is not the oil, it is not the laying on of hands by the elders, it is not the faith, nor is it even prayer in some sort of magical sense. It is God who heals.

Some people have done a great disservice to healing ministries by making people feel that healing depends on the faith of the one asking to be healed. One of the cruelest statements we can make when someone is not healed is "It's because you did not have faith." Healing does not depend on our faith. It is a gracious gift of God.

When the sick call upon the elders of the church to anoint them with oil and pray, the usual expectation is that God will perform a miracle of healing—an intervention. In 1983 I began to share with our elders what the Scriptures taught about the authority and responsibility God had given us as leaders in his church to pray for healing for people under our care. Shortly thereafter, we began monthly healing services at Sunset. During these services of prayer and healing, we invite people to come forward to request physical, emotional or spiritual healing. When people come, pastors, lay pastors or elders anoint them with oil and pray for them. Some of the elders were a bit hesitant about engaging in this ministry, but as they saw people healed and received letters of thanks from people who had been healed, they gained confidence that God really could use them in this ministry.

A few years later, I received this letter from one of our attenders.

Dear Pastor Ron,

In the past two years I have attended two healing services for my mother who has twice attempted suicide. She has a long history of mental and emotional problems. For over a year she lived at a residential care center. Today, thanks to your healing services, she is at home with my dad again. She is functionally well and going for marriage counseling with my dad as well as individual counseling for herself.

I am thankful that Sunset offers healing services. Although I kept my mom in prayer daily, the healing service provided me with another important way of petitioning God on my mother's behalf. Over a year ago I was afraid that my mom would never be well enough to come home. Today I am thankful that I didn't limit God's healing power when I prayed. Thank you, Ron, for the healing services at Sunset. They met my mom's need for healing as well as my need to feel I was doing all that I could as I prayed for her. The support of others in prayer is so powerful.

Interaction

When we pray for God to heal, usually we are requesting a miraculous intervention. But that is not the only way God works. Another way God heals is through what we might call an interaction. In this case, God doesn't reach down and rescue us or miraculously heal us but meets our need by energizing us with the strength or wisdom we need to solve our own problem. Ultimately, we achieve the same result. We are healed. But the healing may require a period of time to be accomplished.

We find a biblical example in Philippians 4:13: "I can do everything through him who gives me strength." Christ doesn't do it for me; I do it with his help. Jesus shows us another example of this in his Great Commission: "Again Jesus said, 'Peace be with you! As the Father has sent me, I am sending you.' And with that he breathed on them and said, 'Receive the Holy Spirit'" (Jn 20:21). Christ tells us to go out and make disciples. He doesn't do it for us. He accomplishes it by empowering us to go out.

James describes a miraculous intervention when he says, "Prayer offered in faith will make the sick person well" (Jas 5:15). He describes an interaction, however, when he goes on to call us to take steps to assist in our healing: "If he has sinned, he will be forgiven. Therefore confess your sins to each other and pray for each other so that you may be healed. The prayer of a righteous man is powerful and effective" (Jas 5:15-16).

The Bible does not teach that there is an inevitable connection between sin and illness, but James suggests that at times this may be the case. Modern medicine has discovered that illness is often a product of wrong living, as in cases of psychosomatic illness. When people come for prayer and healing, we ask them to tell us about the onset of their sickness so that we can ascertain if sin might be the cause of their illness.

Since our physical or emotional problems can be related to moral issues in our lives, James tells us to confess our sins to each other. He's talking about public confession of sin. We intuitively recognize this need for confession, so we've created a mechanism—professional counseling—whereby we can pay for the privilege of confessing our sins. Confession before other people is often an essential step we need to take in order to break from sin and discover deep healing.

When God heals through an interaction, the healing usually occurs gradually. His answer to our prayers may come in the form of enabling us to find good physicians to cure us through medication, therapy or surgery. Or he puts us in touch with the right church, pastor or counselor who can help us find healing spiritually or emotionally. God's response to our prayers may involve a combination of faith and medicine.

After one of our monthly healing services, a woman who experienced healing gave her testimony in a Sunday-morning worship service:

I come before you this morning because I have a new belief in prayer. A few months ago I was sitting in the pew as you are today. I was enjoying the fine music and listening to the sermon and was professing my faith in God. I had a cardiac condition and suffered from diabetes, but in general, my life was going well.

Then something happened. I had a heart attack. Things looked pretty bleak when my cardiologist brought me the report of my angiogram: "There is nothing we can do. The heart damage is extensive and surgery would be risky." Feelings of helplessness and spiritual dormancy clung to me. I was very sick and terribly discouraged.

I thought of all those Sunday mornings I had professed my faith in God, yet given little thought to earnest prayer. I had never gone forward for prayer during one of the healing services. Was it too late to ask God for help? For healing?

I was reassured by our care group leaders as they made their daily visits. I remember saying to them, "I am too weak to pray." Their response was, "We are praying for you. Your family and friends are praying. The care group is praying. The whole church is praying."

As I lay in my hospital bed, I did not realize that there was a power at work much greater than myself and much greater than the medical knowledge of the doctors.

Today, as you can see, I am recovering. My diabetes is in remission. No longer do I take insulin shots. One doctor calls me his "mystery patient." Just this week my cardiologist said to me, "You are a miracle."

I attribute my recovery to prayers of people and to God's healing power. Today, I am conscious of being strengthened and uplifted by the power of prayer. Your prayers have been like a gift to me, the greatest gift known, and in this church I have found the true meaning of the fellowship of believers.

She reported a healing of interaction, for it took place over a period of time and involved the combination of doctors, medication and the loving support of family, pastors and friends.

When we pray for God to heal, we instruct people that they are not to throw away their crutches or stop taking medication until they have been authorized to do so by their physician. We do not ask people to become antimedicine but counsel them to get a medical opinion to confirm if they have really been healed.

One doctor testified that he tried everything he could think of with a particular patient, but nothing seemed to work. It was not until the patient's pastor visited and prayed for healing and for the doctor that the medication he prescribed began to work. Another doctor said, "I believe the greatest healing method of all is the combination of penicillin and prayer."

If you are a physician or a health-care provider, pray for your patients. The healing ministry of the Holy Spirit is not antimedicine, nor should people in the health-care industry scoff at the healing ministry of the church. God heals many people through interaction, a combination of prayer and medical science.

Inner Action

Still another way God heals is through what we call inner action. In this model, God doesn't reach down and remove the problem or sickness. He doesn't give us the power or insight to solve the problem ourselves. He leaves us with our suffering but provides us with an "inner working," the grace to handle our situation and be a witness for him in spite of our circumstances.

The apostle Paul tells us of a time when he prayed for healing. God did not grant his request for an intervention. Nor did he heal him through a process of interaction. Look closely at God's response to Paul's prayer:

> To keep me from becoming conceited because of these surpassingly great revelations, there was given me a thorn in my flesh, a messenger of Satan, to torment me. Three times I pleaded with the Lord to take it away from me. But he said to me, "My grace is sufficient for you, for my power is made perfect in weakness." Therefore I will boast all the more gladly about my weaknesses, so that Christ's power may rest on me. That is why, for Christ's sake, I delight in weaknesses. . . . For when I am weak, then I am strong. (2 Cor 12:7-10)

God did not heal Paul, but he did something wonderful in Paul's life—he provided him with the inner action only God can give. God did not take away his affliction, but he gave him the grace to endure.

Amy Carmichael spent more than fifty years ministering to children in India. The last twenty years of her life she spent in bed, in almost constant pain due to an injury from a severe accident. Yet it was during these years that she did all her writing—poems, devotional books and accounts of the ministry of the Dohnavur Fellowship. These books continue to minister to thousands of people throughout the world, though she has long since gone to be with the Lord. Had she not been confined to her bed, she would never have taken the time to write. Though confined to bed, she had a grace about her that made her a powerful witness.[3]

Charlie Wedemeyer was a star football player for the top-ranked Michigan State Spartans in the mid-1960s. But Charlie no longer has the use of his once-speedy legs. That's because he is confined to a wheelchair as a result of amyotrophic lateral sclerosis, or Lou Gehrig's disease. ALS, which is a degenerative disorder that attacks the body's neuromuscular system, has left Charlie, age forty-three, quadriplegic. He is unable to move the muscles below his neck.

Two women accompany Charlie wherever he goes: his wife Lucy and one of three nurses who tend him in round-the-clock shifts. Unable to breathe on his own, he is totally dependent on a respirator. His neck muscles have atrophied to the point where he can no longer speak. Lucy or his chief nurse, Linda Peevyhouse, serve as his interpreters: he mouths the words as they translate his messages. In spite of the deterioration of his outer body, Charlie is as witty and tenacious as he ever was—probably more so. The disease has not affected his brain, thus leaving his sharp, lively mind captive in an inactive body.

Have the Wedemeyers given up hope? No. Twelve years ago Charlie was told that he had a fatal disease and that he would be dead within three years. Despite the overwhelming odds, Charlie and Lucy—who met and fell in love twenty-five years ago at Punahou High School in Honolulu—used the potential liabilities of Charlie's disease to reach thousands of others in need.

Though Charlie is no longer a varsity head football coach, he is still actively involved on the freshman-sophomore level. He also gives talks—via Lucy and Linda—two or three times a week at Bible studies, churches, schools and camps. He tells teens, "Tomorrow when the alarm goes off and you don't want to get up, just be glad you can get out of bed by yourself."

Recently Charlie, Lucy and Linda recorded a broadcast for *Focus on the Family*. James Dobson asked this question: "Charlie, do you realize that it is possible that you will touch more lives through your illness than you ever did through your athletic ability?"

"For years," responded Charlie, "I prayed to the Lord, 'Heal me.' Now, I simply pray, 'Use me.' " Without a doubt, God is honoring Charlie's prayer.[4]

It is a dangerous misunderstanding of the Bible to say categorically that it is God's will that everyone be well. Sometimes God in his wisdom determines that he can bring more glory to himself through an illness than through a healing. A member of our church has spent much of his life in a wheelchair or moving about with the assistance of a walker. He tells me that he does not believe that it is God's will for him to be healed, for then he would have less of a ministry to the disabled community. He gets frustrated when people insist that God's will can only be for him to be healed.

Have you ever considered that, quite possibly, you could have a greater witness for Christ in a wheelchair than as an All-American athlete? Or that you can attract more people to the Savior through cultivating a cheerful attitude in the midst of an illness than by being free of all sickness and pain? God has not promised to heal us every time we ask. Sometimes his will is not that we be set free from ill-health but that, by God's grace, we learn to persevere in spite of a debilitating illness. We call this the inner action of God—another way God heals.

The Last Word

The prophet Isaiah writes, "Those who hope in the Lord will renew their strength. They will soar on wings like eagles; they will run and not grow weary, they will walk and not be faint" (Is 40:31). Isaiah is showing us that God works in different ways with people. Some people are given the adventure of flying like eagles. They experience the intervention of God, his miraculous healing touch. Others discover the enabling of God to run and not grow weary. They are blessed with the interaction of God. Still others find the grace of God sufficient to help them walk but not faint. They are recipients of the inner action of God.

It's always God's will to heal, but we cannot be certain in which way he will heal. You may still wonder why when we pray with faith, God does not answer our prayers for healing in the way we have presented them to him. This is an important question, so I will devote the next chapter to it.

Questions for Reflection and Discussion

1. If God does not instantaneously heal when we pray for healing, then he has not answered our prayer for healing. Do you agree or disagree with this statement?

2. What do you believe concerning prayers for healing?

3. Do you find it helpful to consider the different ways God heals: by intervention, interaction and inner action? How?

How else might God heal?

4. Read James 5:13-16. What does God promise in this passage? What is not promised?

5. What principle or insight in this chapter was most helpful to you?

TEN

Praying with Faith

◆

RECOGNIZING that God heals in different ways helps us better understand why some people who pray for healing are healed and others are not. Our inquiry does not end here, however. We're still left wondering why when we pray with faith, God does not answer our prayers in the way we have presented them to him.

Does the Bible not teach that whatever we ask for in faith, we will receive?

The prayer offered in faith will make the sick person well. (Jas 5:15)

I tell you the truth, anyone who has faith in me will do what I have been doing. He will do even greater things than these, because I am going to the Father. And I will do whatever you ask in my name, so that the Son may bring glory to the Father. You may ask me for anything in my name, and I will do it. (Jn 14:12-14)

His promise is incredible. He says if we have faith, we can do greater things than he did. When he prayed for people to be healed, in practically every case they were healed instantaneously. Do these verses mean that if we have enough faith, we can expect immediate and dramatic results nearly every time we pray?

Not necessarily. Although Scripture teaches that God always answers when we pray with faith, this isn't the only truth we need to grasp. The apostle John is of help here: "This is the confidence we have in approaching God: that if we ask anything according to his will, he hears us. And if we know that he hears us . . . we know that we have what we asked of him" (1 Jn 5:14-15).

God doesn't grant anything we ask simply because we believe. Just because I believe God is going to make me into the world's greatest basketball player doesn't mean I'm going to threaten Hakeem Oloujawan or Michael Jordan. I must ask in God's will. Only when we know what we ask is in God's will can we be certain we'll receive it.

Putting Jesus' and John's words together we have the whole truth: If we know that what we ask is in God's will and if we pray with complete faith, we will receive what we ask. John's epistle helps us interpret John's Gospel. Jesus meant that we will receive those requests that we ask in faith, if they are presented in Christ's name. Praying in Jesus' name is synonymous with praying in God's will. We interpret these two passages to mean that we are to pray in faith, but we cannot have absolute faith unless we know God's will. Stated differently, the only time we can pray with complete faith that God will answer is when we know that what we ask is in God's will. This helps us discover an important principle for understanding God's will in healing or any other prayer: *God always answers the prayer of faith, but we cannot pray with complete faith unless we know that our request is in God's will.*

Jorie told me that during her first husband's terminal illness one of the hardest things to handle was the guilt heaped on her by well-meaning but misguided Christians who said, "He could be healed if you just have enough faith." Friend, one thing I can tell you with certainty is that healing does not depend on your faith. It's totally up to God. You cannot pray with total faith unless you know with certainty that it is God's will to graciously heal.

When we suggest that anyone can be healed if they have enough faith, we wrongly place our emphasis on a person's faith. Instead, our confidence can and must be only in God. Healing depends on him. It is an act of his grace. But we can pray with complete faith only when we are certain that what we request is God's will.

It is always right and proper to pray for miraculous physical or emotional healing, but we can have complete confidence that God will intervene only when we are absolutely certain God will receive the most glory through healing. In some cases we may surmise that God will be pleased to grant our prayer for healing because we are quite certain that a person can draw more people to Christ through continued life than in death. But seldom can we make such a request with absolute faith.

I recently conducted a memorial service for a member of our church who passed away after a two-year battle with cancer. We prayed for his healing numerous times. Yet in spite of our prayers, God took him to heaven. A few days after his death, his godly wife, who dealt with his passing remarkably well, commented to me, "Although I am really sad that he is gone, I have to admit that God may have received more glory through his death than through his life." Her husband had been quiet about his faith during his lifetime. During his illness, however, he became more outspoken about his faith. His quiet serenity in the face of death was a powerful testimony to his friends and associates.

It Never Hurts to Ask

Even though we cannot be certain when and how God will heal, we can know that God always wants us to ask for healing. It is not always God's will to miraculously heal, but it is always God's will for us to ask. Jesus said, "Ask and it will be given to you; seek and you will find; knock and the door will be opened to you. For everyone who asks receives; he who seeks finds; and to him who knocks, the door will be opened" (Mt 7:7-8).

Jesus' message is clear. God invites us to ask. It's never wrong to ask. This is another essential principle concerning God's will for healing: *Although we cannot presume when and how God will heal, God always invites us to pray for healing.* The same can be said of all our requests in prayer.

Get into the habit of asking God regularly for healing for yourself, family members, fellow church members, friends and associates. When you visit a sick friend in the hospital, lay your hands on him or her and pray. If you have a difficult time believing that God will grant healing, ask God to increase your faith. When family members are sick, place your hands on them and ask God to heal. God wants us to ask.

When our oldest son was twelve years old, he had his tonsils removed. Following the surgery, Jorie and I brought him home. We watched helplessly as he complained of severe discomfort in his throat and ears. We gave him the pain medicine the doctor had prescribed, but other than that we didn't know what else to do.

Jorie suggested that we pray. We laid hands on his throat and ears and prayed in the name of Jesus for God to deliver him from pain. His pain went away immediately.

God did not grant complete healing, however. A couple of hours later Tad called for us to lay hands on him again and pray for Jesus to take away the pain. Numerous times during the next twenty-four hours, we were called to Tad's side for prayer. Each time God took away the pain. Our prayers were not in lieu of medical care. We still gave Tad pain syrup. But our prayers were a critical part of our son's care.

When illness strikes, pray. If your church has a healing service, give God an opportunity to show his grace by attending and asking for prayer. Scripture promises special authority to church leaders in the realm of healing. Out of obedience to Christ, place yourself before the elders of your church, who will anoint you with oil. You may not be absolutely certain of God's will, but it never hurts to ask.

The following true story was recorded in *Guideposts* in July 1989. A physician confessed that he always believed that God worked healing only through the hands of health professionals and the miracles of modern medicine. But he learned otherwise.

He was called to a patient in Newcastle-upon-Tyne, England, one chilly morning. His patient, Alfred Lawrie, had only a few days to live. His preliminary examination showed him to be suffering from heart failure and severe bilateral bronchopneumonia complicated by asthma. His legs, sacrum and lungs indicated retained fluid, his pulse throbbed spasmodically, and his blood pressure was dangerously low. His temperature read 102.5 degrees. He had several medical problems, any one of which could kill him.

Lawrie refused to go to the hospital. As the doctor put on his coat, Mrs. Lawrie informed him that her husband had a great distrust of hospitals. "In fact, you are the first doctor he has ever seen in his life. And then he only let us call you because you were a Christian."

The doctor's only option was to set up a home-care procedure: intravenous digoxin and aminophylline for the man's heart and asthma, oxygen to help his breathing and injections of penicillin for the pneumonia.

As the physician drove on to his next patient, Mrs. Lawrie's words rang in his mind: "because he heard you were a Christian." What difference could his being a Christian make to Lawrie? The penicillin and other treatment he gave him would have been as effective if he had been an atheist. Suddenly a thought came to him quite unexpectedly: *You can pray for him to be healed.* The idea startled him. Although he had accepted Jesus as his Lord and Savior, his firm conviction was that miracles were wrought by God to get his church going, but we have penicillin today, and that is miracle enough.

However, when Lawrie's blood report came back, it was obvious that he needed more medical help than penicillin. His night nurse reported that she had not been able to administer treatment that morning and added, "I don't think he'll last more than an hour."

The doctor drove immediately to Lawrie's house. Here's his story in his own words:

Why, oh why, Lord, can't we help him? I found myself praying. Again the thought came: *You can pray for him to be healed.* As I stood there looking at this ill man, words from the Gospel of Mark ran through my mind like a message on a theater marquee: *These signs shall follow them that believe; in my name shall they . . . lay hands on the sick, and they shall recover.* With the night nurse looking at me anxiously, I faced my own crisis, just as Mr. Lawrie was facing his.

Then with the uncertainty of Peter climbing over the rail of that boat on the Sea of Galilee, I climbed over my own threshold of faith. Hesitant to pray openly, I visualized myself laying hands on Mr. Lawrie as I silently and awkwardly prayed: "Lord, in the name of Jesus, heal this man. He belongs to you. I don't believe he should die now, please heal him."

Mr. Lawrie lay still, his eyes closed, almost in a coma. Mrs. Lawrie and her daughter had come into the room, and I turned to them. "I've done all I can," I said huskily.

Something kept drawing me back to the Lawrie house. After an hour I returned, wondering if my patient was still alive. He was. He did not appear improved, and his breathing was strained, but he was alive! Two hours later I returned again. Mrs. Lawrie met me at the door. Was there a hint of relief in her eyes? Upon examining her husband, I found his color better. His breathing was still labored, but his pulse had steadied.

It turned out to be the strangest day in my practice as I returned to the Lawrie house hour after hour, fascinated by Mr. Lawrie's progress. That evening I was surprised to find him sitting in a chair beside his bed. He was still a very ill man, but now very much alive. Though I was hesitant about expressing my feelings vocally, I silently gave thanks to God.

Mr. Lawrie continued to improve, and in six months he was back at work in his paper business. He lived another fifteen years.[1]

What if the doctor had been unwilling to ask? After all that has been said, the saddest scenario would be to fail to experience God's healing power simply because we fail to ask. You may not know when or how Christ will answer your prayers. You may even lack faith. But you know Christ has the power to heal. So ask him.

Even though lots of people have been healed through Sunset's healing ministry, some elders and lay pastors confess trepidation about praying for people to be healed. If you share their apprehension, it may help you to know that once, in a transparent moment, a popular contemporary faith healer acknowledged that his results, if analyzed carefully, could only claim about a 10 percent success rate. This brings miracle-working closer to our level. Nobody bats a thousand. It's okay to keep on asking and believing even if we strike out nine times out of ten. In fact, it's not only okay, it's essential. Without stepping up to the plate, without asking, we wouldn't even get one out of ten.[2]

Authoritative Prayers

When speaking of praying with faith, we must address authoritative prayers. Ordinary forms of prayer proceed from earth to heaven. We ask for forgiveness, give thanks or request that God meet some need. To use a spatial image, it is prayer *upward*.

But often prayers for healing move in the opposite direction. They need to be authoritative prayers. We are bringing the resources of heaven to bear upon a particular health problem. It is prayer *downward*. In authoritative prayer we call forth the will of God upon the earth. We do not ask God to do something; rather, we use the authority of God to command something to be done.

Jesus prayed this way and urges us to do the same. Once, when he encountered a large crowd, Jesus found that his disciples had been of no help to a father whose son was demon-possessed. After listening to the father's plea for help, and "when Jesus saw that a crowd was running to the scene, he rebuked the evil spirit. 'You deaf and mute spirit,' he said, 'I command you, come out of him and never enter him again.' The spirit shrieked, convulsed him violently and came out" (Mk 9:25-26).

Jesus did not talk to God at all. He spoke directly to the demonic spirit, commanding it to leave. This is a prayer of command. This kind of prayer is peppered all through Jesus' ministry. To blind eyes he said, "Be opened." To lepers he ordered, "Be clean." He compelled the wind and waves with "Quiet, be still!"

Authoritative prayers are focused primarily against the principalities and powers of darkness. Often physical, emotional and spiritual health problems are caused by unseen spiritual forces of evil, so our prayers need to be directed against enemies behind the illness. We speak directly to the spirits or the pain or the infirmity in the name of Jesus.

Some time ago, our fourth son, Joel, suffered from a painful ear infection. He had seen the doctor and received medication, but he was finding no relief. So I prayed, "Lord, we are providing Joel with the best medical attention we can. But he is still in pain. We command you, pain, in the name of Jesus, to be gone. Now!" Instantly Joel's whining and fussing stopped. He laid his head on my shoulder and fell asleep. It happened so abruptly, it startled me. When he awoke later that day, his infection was gone.

Edward Murphy travels the world with Overseas Crusades. In India he occasionally works with an evangelist named Patro, a strong proponent of power encounters. Patro and his team will enter a hostile Hindu village, call out the village priest and say loudly, "The God of Jesus Christ is the only true and living God—a God of power. Bring us the sickest person in your village." When they do, Patro prays for healing in public, and when the person is healed, hearts are quickly opened to the gospel.[3]

Since Satan is the author of sickness, we should pray against the spiritual forces of evil when praying for healing, particularly when we sense that an illness may be related to demonic activity. Even without evidence of demonic activity, authoritative prayer is appropriate, for we're treading on Satan's territory when we deliver people from sickness. It is God's will for us to claim enemy territory, so he wants us to pray for healing. We cannot be certain when and how God will respond to our prayers for healing, but it is always his will for us to ask.

Questions for Reflection and Discussion

1. Suppose someone prays with total faith that a friend be healed, but the person is not healed. As a result, the person begins to question Jesus' promise in John 14:12-14. How would you explain this promise to the person?

2. Read 1 John 5:14-15. What kinds of things can we pray for with total faith?

3. When can we pray for healing with total assurance that God will answer our prayers?

4. Read James 5:13-16 and Matthew 7:7-11. Do you agree that we should pray for healing more frequently than most of us do? Why or why not?

ELEVEN

Praying to Discern God's Will for a Group Decision

◆

SOME time ago an incident took place on a seminary campus that illustrates one of the most important spiritual dilemmas of our time. A number of people of various Christian denominations were participating in a continuing education event addressing the church's response to community problems. The conferees were given a controversial case study and asked to decide, along denominational lines, how they would respond. The groups met separately and then reported back to the total conference. The United Church of Christ group reported that it would appoint a task force to work out a strategy to be voted on by the congregation; the Episcopal group announced that it would present the controversy to its vestry and ask for a decision; the Roman Catholic group announced that it would present the problem to its bishop for a ruling on how to proceed.

After much discussion, a black Baptist pastor of a rapidly growing storefront congregation stood up to make his report. "I don't understand where you all are coming from with all your talk about committees, strategies and task forces. In our church I would call all the deacons together and we would lock ourselves in a room and we would stay there praying until the answer came."

Everyone laughed, but it was nervous laughter. For in the silence of their hearts they were all musing over the disturbing possibility that they had been told something they very much needed to hear. The storefront pastor had been talking about how a group prays for guidance and discerns God's will.

Thus far we have discussed how individuals can discern God's will for their life through prayer. There are also times when a group seeks to understand the will of God corporately. Decisions to acquire new property, to fire a staff member, to hire a new president or CEO, or to move in a new direction in ministry are usually group decisions. As difficult as it may seem to determine God's will for you individually, group decision-making is even more complex. How can we discern God's will for a group decision?

Power in Group Unity

The place to begin is to achieve group unity. The power unleashed when Christians who agree about God's will for their ministry come together in prayer is so awesome that it is worth the effort to reach such concord. When we face difficulties in bringing a board or staff to agreement over a given issue, we may be prone to sigh in frustration: "Oh well, I guess we can never expect everyone on our team to agree as to what we should do." Although I recognize that it is nearly impossible to get everyone to agree on every issue, I do believe it is worth our effort to press for group consensus as to God's will for an organization.

Jesus said, "I tell you that if two of you on earth agree about anything you ask for, it will be done for you by my Father in heaven" (Mt 18:19). God promises power in our prayers when we make the effort to come to agreement about God's will for us before we pray. Such a synergy of power is created when a group achieves unanimity.

I believe it is worth whatever toil it takes to bring the body to concurrence as to God's will for their ministry.

In Acts 4 we see an example of the power available to us when Christians agree on God's will for them. The apostles had collided with the Sanhedrin, a confrontation brought on by a miraculous healing. The Sadducees, angered by Peter's talk of resurrection, grabbed Peter and threw him in jail.

The next day the Sanhedrin, after threatening Peter and John and commanding them not to preach in the name of Jesus, released them. Peter and John returned to the gathered believers and related the story. What was the young church's reaction? Did they try to establish a dialogue with the Sanhedrin or organize a protest march against religious discrimination? Did they search for someone with friends in high places to reason with the authorities? No. They went to their knees: "When they heard this, they raised their voices together in prayer to God" (Acts 4:24), for they were in agreement that it was not God's will for them to stop preaching Christ.

"Why do the nations rage
   and the peoples plot in vain?
The kings of the earth take their stand
   and the rulers gather together against the Lord
   and against his Anointed One."

Indeed Herod and Pontius Pilate met together with the Gentiles and the people of Israel in this city to conspire against your holy servant Jesus, whom you anointed. They did what your power and will had decided beforehand should happen. Now, Lord, consider their threats and enable your servants to speak your word with great boldness. Stretch out your hand to heal and perform miraculous signs and wonders through the name of your holy servant Jesus. (Acts 4:25-30)

The church prayed with agreement about God's will for them. "After they prayed, the place where they were meeting was shaken. And they were all filled with the Holy Spirit and spoke the word of God boldly" (Acts 4:31). God shook the building as a supernatural demonstration of his pleasure with their prayer. God filled them with his Holy Spirit so they could speak his Word with boldness.

We offer powerful prayers when we pray for things we know are in God's will: "This is the confidence we have in approaching God: that if we ask anything according to his will, he hears us" (1 Jn 5:14). Frequently, I ask before we pray if members in the group agree that a request is in God's will. If they do, I know we can pray with confidence.

The body of Christ has far more authority than it knows. Remember the order: agree on God's will, pray for God's will, receive God's power. United prayer is the secret weapon of the church.

History shows that a renewed commitment to corporate prayer has preceded all great revivals. Prayers by God's people fill the atmosphere with such an obvious presence of God that people know he is there. Prior to the Welsh revival of 1904, Christians were convinced that it was God's will for them to pray for church renewal. During the movement of the Spirit, it was reported that strangers entering the villages unaware of the awakening would suddenly fall under deep conviction and seek out a minister to pray for them. Fishermen, drawing near to shore, again unaware of what was happening among the Christians in Wales, would come under terrible conviction of sin, and before their feet touched land, every man on board would be converted. The revival swept like a tidal wave over Wales, and a hundred thousand people were converted and joined churches in a five-month period.

The Three-Step Process

How can we experience this power through prayer? How can a group come to a consensus concerning God's will for them? We need to engage in a corporate process of agreeing on God's will for a group. This discernment process is not needed for most decisions. Closure can be brought to most discussions by a simple vote and call for consensus. But when there are two good options and there is no clear consensus as to which way God is leading, taking time to engage in the discernment process is well worth the energy expended. Let me suggest a three-step process.[1]

1. *Personal preparation.* For a group to discern God's will, each individual in the decision-making process must make four commitments.

First, each person must have an intense desire to know and to do God's will. If an organization is to find God's will, the individuals within the organization must want to do God's will. Everyone must be committed and open to doing God's will, whatever that may be. For this to be possible, everyone involved in the decision-making must share a common allegiance to Christ.

The average worship attendance was no more than twenty-five the year before I came to Sunset Church in 1981. I did inherit, however, a full nine-member elder board. We had some interesting disagreements at the board meetings during my first few months at Sunset. A new pastor working with a previously established board has all the makings for conflict. But I am certain that one of the reasons we had difficulties was that not all the elders shared a common vision for the church. A common faith and vision are essential for an organization to discover God's will.

I find that the best way to begin the discernment process is for the entire group to spend a significant amount of time in prayer. I try to begin all meetings with a season of prayer. While we are praying I invite people to lead us in Scriptures or hymns of praise or songs of confession so that we come clean before God. As we bathe ourselves in God's presence, the desire to do God's will alone increases. Things begin to change not when we study about prayer, not when we talk about it, not even when we believe in it, but when we actually pray. For this reason, I attempt to start meetings with as much as forty-five minutes devoted to prayer.

I usually direct the group to pray about the issue at hand or one subject at a time. Group prayer is stronger when we pray about one subject at a time. Whether you are praying as a group or divided into small groups, you're more likely to pray in one accord when a leader suggests that you move from one topic to another. When one person is praying aloud, others are praying silently on the same subject. In this way everyone is praying together instead of planning other prayers in advance.

Second, each person must cultivate trust in God's willingness to guide. We have no reason to doubt God's willingness to guide. He wants us to know his will so that we can obey him. He does everything he can to make his will perfectly clear to us. Everyone in the group-discernment process must trust that God will guide his people.

After I had been at Sunset Presbyterian Church for ten years, it became increasingly clear to most of our staff and elders that we were running out of room and we would need to look for property elsewhere if the church was to continue to grow. We assigned our long-range planning commission to study what our options were and present them to the board. After a year of study, we determined that we should focus all our future planning on finding new property and stop adding new buildings to our present property. Yet as the months went by, we found that it was difficult to convince the entire congregation of our need to move. Once we garnered congregational support for moving, we found that it was equally difficult to locate new property. At times we wondered where and how God was leading us. We had to constantly remind ourselves of God's willingness to guide.

Third, each person must have an indifference to all but God's will. Each member must set aside his or her own personal agenda and be desirous of doing God's will alone. We can cultivate this indifference only when we are convinced that God's way is always best. To help prepare, I usually lead us in a Bible study that shows that God's will is always best and that he wants us to discover it.

Fourth, each person must experience freedom from prejudgments about the issue. If we are to be open to God's leading, each person must make every effort to enter the process with an open mind. Group discernment cannot take place if people come to the table with their minds already made up.

2. *Group preparation.* Now we are ready to engage in group preparation for discernment. Three things need to happen during the group preparation stage.

First, agree upon the primary purpose of the group. For a Christian organization to function effectively it must have a clear mission statement that clarifies the purpose of the ministry. Everyone in the organization must know what the organization is trying to accomplish. Clearly defined purpose reduces conflict and builds morale. When people know up front where a ministry is going, everybody is working for the same purpose.

One of the first things I did when I came to Sunset Presbyterian was to develop a church purpose statement. Mission statements are difficult for an organization to write, but they are well worth the effort. We updated it in 1994. Both times it required hard work. The vision statement, which includes the dreams and philosophy of Sunset, is nine pages in length. Our brief mission statement reads as follows:

Sunset Presbyterian Church exists to make disciples of Jesus Christ through worshiping God with passion, reaching out to unchurched people with diligence, and nurturing God's people with love.

Agreeing on the primary mission of your group is of immense help to you if you are trying to ascertain God's will for you. Your vision statement tells you what is your business and what is none of your business. As you contemplate a particular action, you can ask yourselves, "Will this program help us fulfill our purpose?" If it does, you do it. If it doesn't, you don't.

You cannot experience united prayer unless there is agreement among those with whom you pray as to what you are trying to accomplish. There have been times when Jorie and I have disagreed, and I say, "Let's pray." She declines. I say, "What's the matter? Don't you want to pray to God?" She says, "No, I don't want to pray with you." You can't pray with someone with whom you are out of sorts. It doesn't work. That's why the apostle Paul says, "Make every effort to keep the unity of the Spirit through the bond of peace" (Eph 4:3). We must be in unity and agree on our purpose if we are to experience power in corporate prayer.

Members of the early church could lift their voices to God because they enjoyed a harmony of fellowship: "All the believers were one in heart and mind. No one claimed that any of his possessions was his own, but they shared everything they had" (Acts 4:32). This is the kind of praying that shakes a place—when God's people come together with one heart to recognize Jesus as Lord. When all our different concerns are thrust aside and our hearts flow into one main street, that's when the presence of God is manifested and people know that God has taken the field.

Following his conversion in 1929, C. S Lewis wrote to a friend: "When all is said about divisions of Christendom, there remains, by

God's mercy, an enormous common ground." We must lay aside our differences with regard to nonessentials and emphasize our common ground.

Second, formulate genuine alternatives; discard those that are weak. At this stage, we need to throw out all the alternatives that are clearly inadequate. We can use conventional group methods of discussion and voting to accomplish this. The discernment process is used to help a group decide between two good choices. When one is not clearly better than the other and there is uncertainty as to which would be the wisest way to go, we need to engage in the discernment process.

When our long-range planning commission made its report to the session in the fall of 1992, it presented us with three options: (1) Add buildings and parking to our present site and continue to enjoy some measure of growth. (2) Purchase a new site where we could pursue unlimited growth. (3) Make planting new churches our primary means of dealing with growth.

We eliminated option 3, since planting churches is a difficult process in the Presbyterian Church U.S.A. We did not feel that this was the best way to handle our growth. Furthermore, studies show that when mother churches plant new churches, God quickly replaces the members who left to start the new ministry, so it may not solve the growth problem at all. We have helped plant two churches and will plant more in the future, but that is not our primary plan for dealing with future growth. That left us with two options, to stay where we are or move to a new site.

Third, each person becomes informed about the alternatives. No one can make a good decision based on ignorance. Each person must be fully informed about the alternatives. I agree with General George Patton, who said, "Every decision is easy once you have all the facts."

This past year our presbytery approved an avowed, practicing homosexual to begin the process of preparation for ordination to the gospel ministry. They did this in spite of the fact that the General Assembly of the Presbyterian Church U.S.A. has voted overwhelmingly several times in recent years against the ordination of homosexuals. Evangelicals in our presbytery were offended that a committee would put forward a candidate for the possibility of future ordination whom the Scriptures and the General Assembly declare to be unsuited for the ministry. Our church was one among a dozen churches in our presbytery that voted to withhold their per capita giving in protest. Our united protest caught the attention of the presbytery because our combined withholding represented 25 percent of its budget.

After the presbytery spent the year trying to win back our trust, our elders took another vote about what we would do with the per capita giving we had withheld and what we would do about next year's giving. When someone called for the question, our board was split down the middle on the issue. That was unusual, for we usually enjoy a high degree of agreement about most things. The uncertainty resulted because we had a lot of unanswered questions. We had no idea what impact our decision would make on the presbytery. If we continued to withhold our money, would it increase our ability to effect change in the presbytery or decrease our impact? If we continued our withholding, would the presbytery block our attempts to purchase new property, or was it illegal for them to do so? We decided we could not vote until we had these and other questions answered. We had to be better informed about our alternatives.

As to our decision about moving to a new site, members of the long-range planning commission gave us all an eye-opening education about our two alternatives. We were surprised to learn that we could do some extensive expansion on our present site that would enable us to accommodate quite a bit of additional growth. We could add six hundred seats to our current eight-hundred-seat sanctuary. We could build additional classrooms on top of our current structure. They informed us that we had room to add a gymnasium and fellowship hall to our present property. We also learned that the cost of expanding our present site was nearly as high as moving to a new site where we would have far more growth potential.

The committee identified nearly thirty sites within reasonable proximity to our church's present location that might be available for purchase. Committee members assured us that we could find a buyer for our present facility. With this information about the two alternatives, we were ready for the final step.

3. *The discernment process.* The third step is the actual discernment process. Typically, there are five elements to this process.

First, each person (alone) prayerfully reflects on the alternatives and prepares reasons for supporting each alternative. People can remain seated in the same room with one another, can go off to separate rooms and then come back together, or can be given this as an assignment to report back at the next scheduled meeting. I have used a modification of this process on pastor search committees. If we have narrowed our search to two possible candidates, I ask the committee members to prepare reasons for selecting each possible candidate. I tell them to focus only on the good qualities of each person. Each person will undoubtedly have weaknesses, but I don't want them to bring up negative things at this point. The discernment process works best if we compare only the strengths of each alternative.

Second, the group reconvenes, and each person presents his or her reasons for supporting each alternative. I ask each person to present his or her reasons for supporting an alternative and allow no debate. Questions are allowed only for clarification. It is important that you not allow debate at this point. The process of the group's listening to each person's positive reasons for supporting a position and seeking to understand each person's dialectic without critique will shed new light on the issue without pitting one person's will against another's.

If one person says, "The Lord revealed this to me," I ask the person for a definition of that revelation. Then I ask the group if they are comfortable with that revelation. If the revelation is not from God, we will find that the person is using piety as a cloak for his or her prejudgment of God's will. If the revelation is from God, the discernment process will prove it true.

Third, each person (alone) prayerfully reflects on the reasons presented and prepares his or her conclusion. People are to judge which reasons for each alternative are weightier. They assess which positive reasons for choosing an alternative outweigh the reasons for choosing the other alternative. Then they prepare their conclusions.

As I reflected on the alternatives presented to us by the long-range planning commission, the question that kept coming to me was "Which of these alternatives best helps us fulfill our church's mission statement?" Since 1981 the primary purpose of Sunset has been to reach unchurched people. Sixty-two percent of all the people who have joined our church these past fourteen years have come from unchurched backgrounds. We also know that our church is located in an area of the country where under 20 percent attend church on any given Sunday. The most important reason for supporting the alternative of moving to a new site, it seemed to me, was that it better helped us fulfill Christ's commission to "go and make disciples" (Mt 28:19) of the hundreds of unchurched people we have not yet reached in our community.

Fourth, the group reconvenes, and each person presents his or her prayerful conclusion. Once again, there is to be no debate. This helps avoid pitting one person's will against another's. Discussion is allowed for clarification only.

Fifth, a vote is taken. If consensus is reached, the discernment process is considered complete. By consensus, I do not mean unanimity in the vote. I mean that those who did not vote with the majority consent to going along with the majority. They agree to make it a unanimous vote. If a vote is almost evenly divided, I do not press for consensus. We are not yet ready for consensus. It is only when a small minority are in opposition that I ask if they would be willing to go along with the majority. If so, we have achieved consensus.

When our board voted between expanding our present facilities and searching for new property, I think the vote was 14-2 in favor of seeking new property. We asked the dissenting voters if they would go along with the majority, and they agreed to do so. So we were able to report a unanimous decision to search for new property.

When those voting in the minority refuse to go along with the majority, I hesitate to bring closure on the issue. Although I do not want the majority to be held hostage by one or two dissenters, I also believe that the Holy Spirit can be speaking through the one or two people who have the courage to vote against the majority.

One year I encountered an impasse in seeking God's will for a group decision on a pastoral search committee that taught me even more vividly the importance of respecting the opinions of the minority voters. The committee had read scores of résumés, interviewed more than a dozen people by telephone and made scores of reference calls. We flew three people into town for interviews. We gathered on this particular evening to discuss our prayerful evaluations of the three candidates. We quickly discarded one of them. Then we presented our conclusions regarding the two finalists. After considerable discussion a vote was taken. The tally was 6-3. After further discussion, I asked the three minority votes if they would cast their lot with the majority. Two said they were happy to do so. One would not. We discussed what additional information was needed for him to feel good about extending a call. We assigned some people to do some further reference checking and agreed to table our decision until we made these calls and each member spent more time in prayer.

Later that week, after the reference calls had been completed, I called the lone holdout. "Has any additional information from the calls shed new light to allay your fears about extending a call to this person?" I asked him.

"No," came his candid reply. He did not feel good about proceeding. I did not want a hung committee because of one measly vote. I decided to push for his consent.

"Would you be willing to go with the majority?" I pressed him. "Everybody else feels good about this person." There was stony silence on his end of the line.

"No, I don't think he's the right choice for us." It was my turn for silence.

"Would you be willing to join the committee recommendation if we note your dissenting vote in our report to the session?" I wouldn't give up.

After a long pause he sighed, "All right. I still haven't changed my mind at all. I don't think it is a good decision, but I don't want to hold up the process."

I had won, or so I thought. We called the candidate to serve on our staff. Within months of his arrival it became painfully obvious that we made a mistake. Could it be that the Holy Spirit had been speaking through the one dissenting voter? I realized that if I had not pressed for consensus, we might have avoided this mess.

I learned an important lesson. Don't cut the discernment process short by pressing too quickly for consensus. I realized that it takes a tremendous amount of courage for one person or a few persons to hold out against the majority. Quite possibly the Holy Spirit is speaking to the group through these individuals.

If there are only a handful of dissenting voters and they agree to join the majority, you have achieved consensus. But if one person or a few people refuse to change their vote, then continue the discernment process. Ask people to prayerfully reflect on the evaluations of others and prepare another evaluation report. Continue the process until consensus emerges or the group feels it has gone as far as it can or runs out of time. When we callously disregard the dissenting viewpoints of the minority, we inflict incalculable injury on the group and sow seeds of schism in the body of Christ.

The Last Word

In August and September of 1991, I was invited by the Japanese Church Growth Institute to come to Japan for two weeks to address a group of pastors who wanted to see their churches grow. While I was there I heard about a Japanese church that was experiencing growth problems much like our own. All three of its worship services were already full. What could the members do? They agreed that it was God's will for them to obtain larger facilities. The adjacent downtown property would cost millions of dollars to purchase. Did God want them to move to the suburbs?

They knew that hundreds of thousands of people still needed to be reached in their community. Only one percent of Japanese people today attend church. They simply had to find facilities that would enable them to assimilate more people. They found a perfect piece of vacant land. There was only one problem—the land was owned by a wealthy doctor who refused to sell.

So what did they do? For one week, at the end of each workday, the Reverend Uchikoshi and his church elders marched around the desired site, asking God to miraculously release the entire property for sale. Saturday night, the entire congregation marched around the land seven times, singing joyful praises and praying.

Two days later, the recalcitrant owner called the church to say that he was so impressed with the vibrant faith of these Christians that he was now not only willing to sell his property to them but would do so for $100,000 less than what a land developer had offered. They had agreed on God's will, prayed God's will and watched God work.

Questions for Reflection and Discussion

1. Why is it more difficult to discern God's will for a group decision than for an individual decision?

2. Read Matthew 18:19 and Acts 4:31. Why is so much power released when Christians agree on God's will and then pray for God's will?

3. Why is it essential for a Christian organization to have a clear purpose statement if its members are to discern God's will for them?

4. When group members report their evaluations during the discernment process, why is it important that there be no debate?

5. What is the difference between unanimity and consensus?

When dissenting voters refuse to change their vote, why is it important not to press for consensus?

6. What principle or insight in this chapter was most helpful to you?

TWELVE

The Importance
of Praying
in Jesus' Name

◆

BABE Didrikson Zaharias is considered by many to be the greatest woman athlete in history. She set world records in the 1932 Olympics in the eighty-meter hurdles and javelin. But her greatest success came in golf, where she set a record by winning seventeen major tournaments in a row. The Associated Press named her the outstanding woman athlete of the first half of the century.

Some time before Zaharias's untimely death of breast cancer at the age of forty-two, she said, "I have never been what you would call a real churchgoing Christian, but I have always said my prayers which I learned when I was a little child, and I still say the same prayers today."

Interesting. She didn't deal with the rest of her life that way. She didn't have the same golf swing at age forty that she had when she was five. Through sacrifice and self-discipline, she had improved her physical abilities. But at age forty-two she was still praying the same prayers she learned at her mother's knee. Her prayer life was stagnant.

Does that describe your prayer life? Are you praying the same way you did five years ago, or ten or twenty years ago?

I met my wife, Jorie, twenty years ago. When we started dating, I said to her something to this effect: "Jorie, I don't know if you've noticed or not, but I feel something different for you than for the other gals." Suppose now, two decades later, I said the same thing to her. She wouldn't be impressed. We've grown far beyond that kind of dialogue in our relationship.

Likewise, we need to grow in our communication with God. Are you growing in your prayer life? Are you better able to discern God's will for you through prayer than you could five or ten years ago? Take the following test to see if you are growing in prayer. Answer yes or no to these questions:

1. Are you satisfied with your prayer life?

2. Do you feel that your prayers to know God's will are made with more confidence and effectiveness today than they were five years ago?

3. Could you cite four or five answers to requests you have made this past month?

4. Since effective prayer requires that we know God's promises, could you list ten or fifteen promises from God's Word by heart?

5. After you have prayed for guidance, are you confident that God has heard your prayers and will give you the wisdom you need to make a good decision?

6. Since effective praying requires that we pray for things that are in God's will, do you feel you know how to make requests that are in God's will?

If you answered no to one or more of those questions, this chapter is especially for you.

Growing in Prayer

During the past decade, atheistic communism has collapsed throughout most of the Western world. This historic change is as significant as the Reformation or Constantine's conversion. Because it was so vast in its implication, most in North America never seriously thought to pray for the fall of communism. But God heard generalized prayers for revival, and this was one result.

This historic shift is not simply a political victory for democracy; it is the defeat of a demonic power structure that has defied God and persecuted Christians for more than seventy years. You could call it a planetary exorcism, though it has left chaotic and brutal situations—such as the breakup of Yugoslavia—in its wake, as if the demonic forces expelled were seeking new homes built by ethnic and religious hatreds. This shift has opened new avenues of missionary witness throughout the former communist world, where there is a spiritual hunger that puts the West to shame. As my wife and I have traveled in former Soviet bloc countries, we have witnessed a fervency of faith among these Eastern European believers unparalleled among most North American Christians.

Although numerous elements collaborated to bring about the collapse of communism throughout Eastern Europe, no factor was more significant than prayer. In 1983, the Lausanne Prayer Conference for Spiritual Awakening and World Evangelization was held in Korea. The conference brought together prayer movements from all over the world.

People who are most confident about knowing God's will and who are used mightily by God are people who pray. I do not mean those who talk about prayer or can explain how prayer works; I mean those who pray. They have no more time than anyone else. The time is simply taken from something else.

Let's face it. Some people wield far more power in prayer than others. The queen of England once said, "When John Knox prays, my knees shake."

What would she say of your prayers? If you want to discover God's will for you when you pray and experience exciting answers to prayer, you need to learn how to pray.

To suggest that we must learn how to pray leads me to add one caution: I am not suggesting that there is one right way to pray. The first principle of prayer is simply to pray. We learned in chapter eight that we must confess our sins and become transparent before God. Get honest with God and talk to him—often. Any praying is better than no praying.

If you feel confident that you are being led to understand God's will, just keep praying the way you are. But if you are frustrated because your prayers are going unanswered, or you are not experiencing life transformation, or you see no miracles in the lives of people for whom you pray, or you feel that God's leading frequently seems murky, then come with me as we study how to pray.

God assures us that we will find a ready response to prayers offered "in Jesus' name." Read a sampling of Jesus' promises:

I tell you the truth, anyone who has faith in me will do what I have been doing. He will do even greater things than these, because I am going to the Father. And I will do whatever you ask in my name, so that the Son may bring glory to the Father. You may ask me for anything in my name, and I will do it. (Jn 14:12-14)

I tell you the truth, my Father will give you whatever you ask in my name. Until now you have not asked for anything in my name. Ask and you will receive, and your joy will be complete. (Jn 16:23-24)

These verses set forth prayer as the primary human responsibility in the accomplishment of God's program. Divine action depends on believing prayer. Prayer is the chief task of the believer. It is our responsibility to ask. It is God's responsibility to accomplish.

If I had to choose one Bible verse that most succinctly defines the key to praying with power, it would be this promise of Jesus: "I will do whatever you ask in my name, so that the Son may bring glory to the Father" (Jn 14:13). Any thoughtful person knows that praying in Jesus' name must mean far more than just tacking on a rote formula to the end of our prayers. But what exactly does it mean?

Make Requests on Christ's Authority
Praying in Jesus' name means praying on the authority of what Christ accomplished. The name of Jesus is not a secret code that works some kind of magical spell when it is invoked, like "Open Sesame!" It means to pray on Christ's authority. Jesus told us that by virtue of his death

and resurrection God gave him all authority in heaven and on earth (Mt 28:18). To pray in his name means to pray in full assurance of the great work he accomplished—in his life, death, resurrection and continuing reign at the right hand of God the Father. Our prayers have no worthiness apart from Christ's atoning sacrifice. Praying in Jesus' name means to acknowledge our complete helplessness apart from Christ's mediation. It's an appeal to the blood of Christ as the reason we can come before God's throne of grace.

If I go to an out-of-state bank to cash a check I have written for $100, they will say to me, "Mr. Kincaid, we cannot cash this. You don't have an account here." But if my $100 check was signed by a vice president of the bank, they would cash it, no questions asked. Likewise, when I go to the bank of heaven in my own name, I get absolutely nothing, for I have no assets there. But if I go with Christ's name on my checks, I receive whatever I ask, for he has unlimited assets.

If you question how important it is to pray on the authority of Jesus' name, try an experiment. Next time you pray, tell God you are coming in your own name and that you demand to be heard because of all the good things you have done. You will feel utterly impotent. You will realize that you have no authority whatsoever apart from Jesus' name.

When we pray, we can pray with boldness only because of Christ's authority. Christ has already defeated Satan and his demonic horde. The apostle Paul writes of Jesus' victory: "Having disarmed the powers and authorities, he made a public spectacle of them, triumphing over them by the cross" (Col 2:15). You may wonder, "If Satan's defeat is absolute, why do I have such a hard time with him? If the devil is chained, either he has a mighty long chain, or he's chained to me!" That's a good question, and there is a good answer.

Although Satan's defeat is absolute, for the time being—until God brings down the curtain on history—he is still allowed to roam the earth and cause men and women like you and me all sorts of problems. His final doom was sealed at the cross, but at present he fights like a cornered dog to destroy life and take as many people as possible with him.

Our prayers have authority when we pray in Jesus' name, not only because of what he accomplished through his death, but also because he now intercedes for us. Paul writes, "Christ . . . is at the right hand of God and is also interceding for us" (Rom 8:34). The writer to the Hebrews tells us that Jesus "is able to save completely those who come to God through him, because he always lives to intercede for them" (Heb 7:25). Did you realize that Christ intercedes for you? This helps us understand Jesus' promise: "Anyone who has faith in me will do what I have been doing. He will do even greater things than these, because I am going to the Father" (Jn 14:12).

What did Jesus mean when he said we would do greater works than he did? We may find our answer in Luke's narratives in the book of Acts. There are a few miracles of healing, but the emphasis is on the mighty works of conversion. On the day of Pentecost alone three thousand people were added to the little band of believers, more than throughout Christ's entire earthly life. There we see a literal fulfillment of "he will do even greater things." During his lifetime the Son of God was confined in his influence to the comparatively small area of Palestine. After his departure, his followers were able to work in widely scattered places and influence much larger numbers of people.

Jesus made clear that the promise of greater works could be fulfilled only if he returned to the Father. Why? Because upon returning to the Father, he sent the Holy Spirit to reside in all believers. And Jesus himself began to occupy the place of intercession, to hear and answer the prayers of his disciples. We can do greater works because of Christ's prayers for us.

My fifteen-year-old son, David, plays championship tennis tournaments in the Pacific Northwest and around the United States. For a couple of years he was sponsored by Yonex. During that time, he used the Yonex RQ-380 tennis racquet. He had great success with it. Some of his friends bought the racquet simply because he used it.

Monica Seles, the then number-one-ranked player in the world in women's tennis, is the one who made the RQ-380 famous. She was so dominant that some people thought she should be required to play in the men's draw.

I tried the racquet several times. I figured if it could help Monica win the Australian, French and U.S. Opens, it ought to help me with my matches. It didn't. I continued to lose. The truth is, the RQ-380 didn't win the French Open. Monica Seles did. When fans walked away from her matches, they weren't talking about her racquet; they talked about what a fantastic player she was. The type of racquet you use when you play tennis makes a big difference, but it isn't the racquet that wins. It's the champion who wins, using the racquet.

In the work of Christ, Jesus is the champion and we are the racquet in his hands. Christ is the source of power. His atoning sacrifice and ministry of intercession give us the victory. We perform great works only as we allow him to work through us.

By ourselves we have no entrée into the court of heaven. Without Christ, our experience might be analogous to ants trying to speak to humans. They need an intermediary, a go-between. This is what Christ does for us as eternal Intercessor. He grants us access to the throne of grace. Even more, he straightens out our misguided prayers and makes them acceptable before God.

Make Requests That Bring Christ Honor

Praying in Jesus' name also means to make requests that bring Christ honor. It is like saying, "Grant this petition so that Jesus might be magnified." Jesus tells us that he will grant what we ask for in his name so that the Son may bring glory to the Father (Jn 14:13). Anything we ask that will bring honor to the Father through the Son will be granted.

In 2 Kings 19, we find Hezekiah and the people of Judah being taunted by Sennacherib and the commander of the Assyrian army. Sennacherib had conquered all the cities around Jerusalem. He boasted that none of the gods of countries around Judah had been able to deliver their people from him, so why would the fate of Jerusalem be any different? He called for them to surrender. Look carefully at the prayer Hezekiah offered in response:

Give ear, O LORD, and hear; . . . listen to the words Sennacherib has sent to insult the living God.

It is true, O LORD, that the Assyrian kings have laid waste these nations and their lands. They have thrown their gods into the fire and destroyed them, for they were not gods but only wood and stone, fashioned by men's hands. Now, O LORD our God, deliver us from his hand, so that all kingdoms on earth may know that you alone, O LORD, are God. (2 Kings 19:16-19)

Hezekiah was not praying for his own prestige, but for God's name to be honored. He cried, in effect, "Lord, Sennacherib is mocking you. He is claiming that you cannot protect us. He compares you to the other gods he has destroyed, which are no gods at all. God, vindicate your name. Show your power. Save us so that all the world may know that you alone are God." That's good praying, because it has the proper motive. It puts God's honor above everything else.

When I came to be pastor at Sunset in 1981, a non-Christian preschool of about a hundred children rented space from the church. As the church grew and established a Sunday school, we began to need the space that had previously been turned over to the preschool. We began to reassert ownership over our classrooms, and conflicts arose. For example, the preschool teachers did not like the pictures of Jesus or Scripture verses we put up on bulletin boards. They asked us to take them down before their school began on Monday mornings. Our Sunday-school teachers could not believe that they would make such a request of us. It was obvious that the preschool staff was not used to sharing space with an active and growing church.

When we set some new guidelines limiting the amount of space they could use and what they could and could not do in our class-rooms, they began to spread rumors that we were being unfair with them. They made defamatory statements about me and our church board.

I remember praying, "Lord, I don't care what is said about me. Nor am I too concerned with what is said about the elder board. But, Lord, stop these false rumors. Don't let your name be dragged through the mud and people lost from your kingdom whom we otherwise might have reached."

God answered my prayer. Even though they had spread malicious gossip about our church, a number of people who had children in the preschool began to bring their families to our worship services. A few months after the initial conflicts arose, our elders asked the school to relocate the following year. Once it moved out, we experienced peace, and our Sunday school was able to grow without room usage restric-tions.

If you want your prayers answered, make requests that bring honor to Christ. The problem for many of us is that bringing Christ honor is not our primary reason for living.

The Michigan Wolverines' so-called Fabulous Five played in the NCAA Final Four tournament in 1993. After Michigan made a comeback, the camera zoomed in on a Michigan fan holding up a large cardboard sign that said, "THIS IS WHAT WE LIVE FOR." I am often guilty of exaggeration, but this message was beyond belief. Athletic events are often exciting, but they are, after all, only games. I'm glad I have something more important to live for than that.

If your purpose in life is to extend God's kingdom and your requests are needed to carry out his work, your prayers will be answered. If the reason you seek guidance is to know what choice will bring God the most credit, the prayer is likely to be granted. You may object, "I've prayed for things that would bring Christ honor, but he didn't answer." Remember, God always answers in a way and time that will bring him the greatest honor. You may ask for something to bring him glory, but God knows he will receive more glory by waiting to meet your request or by answering in another way.

In recent summers I was asked to speak at the Young Life camp in Malibu, Canada. I took Jorie and our four oldest boys with me. The camp is located on the Princess Louisa Inlet in British Columbia. Since the resort is surrounded by water on three sides, water sports are a big part of the program. The first time we went, our boys were all looking forward to learning how to water-ski. Unfortunately, the weather was cold and cloudy that week, and the water temperature was frigid enough to shock a polar bear. After trying to ski several times, the boys gave up because they got too cold.

When we were getting ready to return the next summer, our thirteen-year-old, David, asked, "Can we get a wet suit?"

"We're not buying a wet suit, David," I informed him.

"Can we borrow one?" He didn't give up.

"No, I'm not going to ask one of my friends if we can borrow his wet suit. I don't like to borrow other people's things." I was firm.

"Why don't you pray for God to provide a wet suit for you?" I counseled him.

David prayed all week long for God to make a wet suit available somehow. When we reached Malibu after an eight-hour boat ride, we were shown to our quarters. After Jorie had been in our cabin for a few minutes, she emerged laughing. "Ron, go look in the closet," she urged.

There I found a wet suit that would fit David perfectly. But although I was delighted, I told Jorie, "We can't take it down to the boat dock. It is somebody else's. We can't use it without permission."

The next day the boys lined up on the dock to take their turns skiing. When it came time for David to ski, I turned to Jorie and said, "Maybe we should let David use the wet suit. He prayed all week for one. It does seem like God provided it for him."

I called to David and told him he could go get the suit. A few minutes later he came trotting down to the dock, grinning from ear to ear, wearing the full-length, green-and-black wet suit. He looked like Lloyd Bridges getting ready for one of his *Sea Hunt* expeditions.

Within a few minutes David had whipped on his skis and was in the water. That day he successfully water-skied for the first time in his life. He was ecstatic. So were we. He was also one mighty pumped kid who knew God answers prayer.

All through the week we asked the Young Life staff if anyone knew who owned the wet suit. Unbelievably, no one did. As we shared our story with more and more staff, many stated their conviction that God had provided the wet suit just for David.

David had made a specific request. God was happy to grant his request, because he knew he would receive the honor.

Make Requests God Has Promised to Grant

Praying in Jesus' name also means to make requests God has promised to grant. When we pray in Jesus' name, we ask for things that further Christ's kingdom. Anything that brings him glory and increases his kingdom is among the things he has promised to grant. Just as schoolteachers love it when students write principles that have been taught during the school year back to them on their test papers, God loves when we recite his promises. When we pray to God for what he has already promised to give, we are assured of receiving what we request of him.

Nehemiah serves as an example. The people of Israel enjoyed their finest years when they were a united kingdom under the leadership of Saul, David and Solomon. Throughout these years God assured the people that if they obeyed him, he would bless them. If they disobeyed, he would scatter them. They chose to disobey. So God sent them into captivity at the hands of the Assyrians and Babylonians. God also promised that if they returned to him, he would restore them to their land.

The book of Nehemiah opens in 445 B.C., some 140 years after the people of Judah were taken into captivity. Nehemiah is living in Susa, the capital of the Persian Empire. His brother has just returned from Jerusalem, and Nehemiah asks him about the welfare of the Jews who have returned to the land of Judah. Learning that the city is a pile of rubble and the walls are still torn down, he mourns for the city and turns to God in prayer.

We don't know all that Nehemiah prays. We have to do some reading between the lines. I imagine he asks God to improve the situation in Jerusalem. I'm certain that as Nehemiah prays, God impresses upon him that he wants him to restore the walls. He asks God to restore the city of Jerusalem and help him rebuild the wall. As you read on in Nehemiah, you find that God answers Nehemiah's prayer and gives him great success.

What makes Nehemiah's prayer so effective? He begins by praising God and confessing Israel's sins, prayer principles we considered in chapters seven and eight. Then he claims one of God's promises from Deuteronomy 30. Look carefully at his prayer.

Remember the instruction you gave your servant Moses, saying, "If you are unfaithful, I will scatter you among the nations, but if you return to me and obey my commands, then even if your exiled people are at the farthest horizon, I will gather them from there and bring them to the place I have chosen as a dwelling for my Name."

They are your servants and your people, whom you redeemed by your great strength and your mighty hand. O Lord, let your ear be attentive to the prayer of this your servant. (Neh 1:8-11)

Nehemiah says, "Lord, you fulfilled the first part. No doubt about it. We were unfaithful and you scattered us among the nations. You did what you said you would do. Now we're claiming the second part of your promise. We are taking your Word seriously, God. Please restore us to our land." He made a strong prayer, because he claimed one of God's promises.

Scripture states clearly that we are to pray about everything and that God will respond to our prayers. That's the way God says it, and that's the way he intends us to take it.

I started keeping a prayer journal my sophomore year in college. Every day I write down ways God has answered specific requests I've made of him. Many of my requests are made on the basis of promises God has made in his Word. As of this writing, I have recorded twenty-two thousand answers to prayer. This journal helps me, particularly in times of crisis. Reviewing the ways God has delivered me in the past gives me confidence that he will help me today.

John Steinbeck, in his book *East of Eden,* writes,

And the dry years would come and sometimes there would be only seven or eight inches of rain. The land dried up and the grasses headed out miserably a few inches high and great bare scabby places appeared in the valley. The live oaks got a crusty look and the cattle listlessly nibbled dry twigs. Then the farmers and the ranchers would be filled with disgust for the Salinas Valley. The cows would grow thin and sometimes starve to death. People would have to haul water in barrels to their farms just for drinking. Some families would sell out for nearly nothing and move away. And it never failed that during the dry years the people forgot about the rich years, and during the wet years they lost all memory of the dry years. It was always that way.[1]

As a Christian, you will face dry times. Cultivating memories of the rich times and how God has fulfilled his promises in the past will sustain you and strengthen your prayers.

Suppose your community experiences a really cold winter and the lake nearest your home freezes over. Someone suggests that you would make a great catch if you did some ice fishing on the lake. You try it, but you don't catch anything because you are afraid that if you walk out to the middle of the lake, the ice will not sustain your weight. Then along comes a real ice fisherman. He walks out to the middle of the lake, sits on a box, chips a hole, begins to fish and catches a bucketful.

Is the ice any stronger for the ice fisherman than for you? No. The difference is in knowledge. He knows ice and where he can walk with confidence. It's the same with prayer. Why do some believers pray with more confidence and authority than others? Because they have a deeper knowledge of God's promises and know what God has already promised to give.

A true story is told of a group of men who had been shipwrecked and were adrift in the Atlantic Ocean in a small lifeboat. The drinking water they had brought with them was gone, and they were dying of thirst. They knew that if they drank the seawater that surrounded them, the salt would only increase their thirst and drive them to madness.

After days of agonizing thirst, a large ship appeared on the horizon, spotted them and came to their rescue. The stranded men cried out through parched lips, "Give us something to drink! Lower some water to us!" One of the sailors on the rescue ship called back, "Take some of the water around you and drink!"

The shipwrecked men thought they were being mocked. But the truth of the matter was this: though they were indeed adrift in the Atlantic Ocean, they were not in salt water but in fresh. They were out of sight of land but were in fact in the mouth of the Amazon River, which is so mighty that where it empties into the ocean, it pushes fresh water hundreds of miles into the sea.[2]

How many of us are like these thirsty sailors? We have come to the cross to claim the forgiveness, peace, love and joy of Christ, but we have not drunk of it. They are all around us, and we do not realize it. Instead we live with guilt, worry, hatred and unhappiness because we do not take what God promised to give us.

What are some of the blessings God promises us? He promises eternal life to those who believe (Jn 3:16). He promises to meet all our needs (Phil 4:19). He promises a way of escape when we are tempted (1 Cor 10:13). He promises to build his church and that the gates of hell will not prevail against it (Mt 16:18). He promises that husbands who love their wives will be blessed, for to love their wives is to love themselves (Eph 5:28).

He promises that it will go well for children who obey their parents (Eph 6:1-3). He promises that we will find our greatest happiness if we serve other people (Jn 13:17). He promises that if we resist the devil, he will flee from us (Jas 4:7). He promises us authority over the spiritual forces of evil (Lk 10:19). He promises to grant wisdom to those who need direction (Jas 1:5).

When we pray for these things, we have assurance that we will receive them, for God has promised to grant these requests. But how can you pray God's promises unless you study the Bible and know what God has promised? The Scriptures contain unsearchable riches, but if we don't know these promises, we live in spiritual poverty.

The original owners of the fabulous Mt. Morgan gold mine in Queensland, Australia, toiled for many years, totally unaware that beneath the ground on which they lived was possibly the richest gold mine the world has ever known. Incalculable riches lay just below the surface, but the people lived in poverty not knowing what they possessed in their land. So it is with Christians who live without claiming the promises God has given them.

Make Requests in God's Will

Praying in Jesus' name also means to make requests in God's will. Nothing asked in the name of Jesus can be contrary to his will. To pray in the name of Jesus is to make requests consistent with his character and purpose. It is as though Jesus himself were making the request. It means we are asking for what he wants. When I want what he wants—when we both want the same thing—we're on praying ground.

As noted earlier, the apostle John writes, "This is the confidence we have in approaching God: that if we ask anything according to his will, he hears us. And if we know that he hears us—whatever we ask—we know that we have what we asked of him" (1 Jn 5:14-15). That's quite a promise. Did you catch the prerequisite? How can we have confidence that we will receive what we ask? By asking in accordance with his will.

One day each week I set aside a two- to three-hour block of time to pray. On one occasion I was praying for church members who have not been coming to church regularly. Pick a church—any church—and thumb through its membership roll. It will surprise you how many people on the rolls are never in church. At one time they attended, but no longer. Christianity is littered with discarded disciples; membership rolls groan under the weight of those who have become bored with following Christ.

But let me ask a question. Are we praying for these people? When we first noticed signs of their losing interest and becoming distracted by the world, when we began to suspect that the enemy was making inroads into their lives—did we pray? Are we praying that God will build a protective wall of grace around them?

I claimed Christ's promise in John 15:16 for these missing members. "I chose you and appointed you to go and bear fruit—fruit that will last. Then the Father will give you whatever you ask in my name." I prayed something like this: "God, you chose us to bear fruit that remains. You don't want us to evangelize people and get them to join our church, only to have them drop out a year or so later. You want us to make disciples who grow to maturity. It's not in your will that people drop out of the faith and stop attending church. I'm aware that some of these people have gone to other churches. But most people, Lord, have simply dropped out. So I ask you to help us minister to and restore these missing people. I will pray for them faithfully and ask our people to do the same."

All of our missing members did not show up the next Sunday, but I believe this was a powerful prayer, because I was praying according to God's will.

When we make selfish requests not in God's will, we cannot hope to have our prayers answered. Like the boy who answered on a test that Paris was the capital of England—when he realized his mistake, he prayed, "Dear God, please make Paris the capital of England."

The key to praying with power is to come to the place where the only things we ask are those which are God's will for us. Our will becomes so transformed that we want only what God wants. Jesus is our example. Before going to the cross, he prayed, "Father, if you are willing, take this cup from me; yet not my will, but yours be done" (Lk 22:42).

Have you come to the place in your life where you can say, "Lord, not my will, but yours be done"? Have you come to the place where all you want is what God wants for you? Prayer, then, is not a matter of changing God's mind so that he will do what we want, but changing us to be conformed to his will.

The Last Word

Pulling these four statements together, we see that praying in Jesus' name means to make requests on Christ's authority, make requests that bring Christ honor, make requests God has promised to grant and make requests that are in God's will. So praying in Jesus' name, for God's honor, according to God's promises and in God's will all mean roughly the same thing. These four statements, by the way, constitute the key qualifiers to powerful praying. God will answer prayers that are prayed in Jesus' name, for they are requests that bring him glory and that accomplish his will.

Watchman Nee was doing an evangelistic tour in a native village where there were no Christians. They arrived January 1 and were preaching around the town, and no one was responding. One of the ministers finally asked the people, "Why don't any of you believe?"

A man responded, "It is because of the god Ta Man Wang. He has never failed us. We have a festival every year on January eleventh, and it never rains on that day, and we believe in him."

The missionary responded, "I guarantee you it will rain on January eleventh!" He and Watchman immediately began to pray. They had some apprehension, but they believed in God. They did not plead with him, but just praised him, because they knew he would come through.

On January 11, they woke up to sunshine and blue sky. During breakfast they were a little frightened, but they reminded God that his honor was at stake in this country. They told him that the gospel would be lost there forever if it did not rain.

As they were finishing breakfast at 8:00 a.m., rain began to fall. The natives brought their god Ta Man Wang out to the streets for a parade. It began pouring in buckets, knocking over the idol and shattering it on the ground.

The natives hurriedly convened a meeting and concluded, "We

must have chosen the wrong day; let's change the date to the four-teenth." So again, Watchman Nee said, "It will rain on the fourteenth." Once again the missionaries went to prayer. On the fourteenth, the town experienced another torrential downpour. Finally the people began to believe. The missionaries witnessed God's power in response to their prayers, because they were praying for something that would bring God glory.

When all we want is for people to know Christ and bring him honor, our prayers will be granted. The power his name has on our lives is the power it will have in our prayers. When his name is everything to us, it will obtain everything for us.

Questions for Reflection and Discussion

1. When people say, "In Jesus' name" at the end of a prayer, do you think it has deep meaning for them, or is it simply a meaningless phrase tacked on to the end of their prayer?

What do *you* mean when you pray "in Jesus' name"?

2. Read Colossians 2:14-15. What did Jesus accomplish that gives his name such authority?

3. Why does God only grant prayers that bring him honor? Why would God not grant requests that do not bring him honor?

4. Make a list of as many promises as you can find in God's Word that he has promised to grant.

5. Read 1 John 5:14-15. What promise does God make?

What are some requests you can make that you are certain are in God's will?

6. What principle or insight in this chapter was most helpful to you?

THIRTEEN

Final Words on Praying for Guidance

♦

THROUGH his Word God has made his grand design plain for all people to understand: that people come to know Christ, become conformed to Christ and seek to share Christ. He wants us not only to know but also to be guided by his grand design. As long as we remain within the boundaries of this grand design, God gives us freedom to make decisions we deem best, and he expects us to take responsibility for these decisions.

The assumption that God has only one choice for us to make in each situation increases the tendency for Christians to rely on circumstantial signs as indicators of God's leading, rather than simply choosing the path that seems most wise. Focusing on making wise choices proves not only a better way to make decisions but also a more biblical approach to decision-making.

Prayer is critical to the process of growing in an understanding of

God's will. Through prayer we begin to discover God's will for us. Through prayer we further God's will and extend God's kingdom on earth as it is in heaven. Through prayer we push back the spiritual forces of evil. Through prayer we praise God, which puts us in the center of God's will for us. Through prayer we confess our sins. This honesty is essential to establishing and maintaining a relationship with God. Through prayer we call forth God's power to heal. Through prayer we are able to listen to God's voice and ascertain his will for an individual or group decision. Through prayer in Jesus' name, we make requests that bring glory to Christ and that God has already promised in his Word to grant.

Through prayer we can live our lives in daily dependence on him, talking to him about all our needs. The fact that we cannot be certain what God's will for us is in all situations causes us to depend even more on him. Although we cannot have total certainty what God's will is, we can still be fully in God's will, for God wills that we share with him our misgivings and uncertainties, fears and anxieties, joys and sorrows, victories and defeats, doubts and questions. He wants us to share everything with him. In short, God wants us to live a life of prayer.

If we are not living in day-by-day submission to the Lord Jesus Christ, we are not partaking in God's will for us at all, for it is God's grand design that all his creatures learn to rely on him for all that they do. As Jesus put it, "Apart from me, you can do nothing" (Jn 15:5). Paul stated it: "This happened that we might not rely on ourselves but on God" (2 Cor 1:9).

There is no better way to rely on God for everything than through a life of prayer. Prayer leads us into God's will and is God's will for us.

Notes

Chapter 1: Finding Our Way out of the "Will-of-God Quagmire"
[1]I am indebted to Garry Friesen and his fine book *Decision Making and the Will of God* (Portland, Ore.: Multnomah Press, 1980) for four of the five points in this critique on the traditional approach to discovering the will of God.
[2]J. I. Packer, *Knowing God* (Downers Grove, Ill.: InterVarsity Press, 1973), pp. 213-14.
[3]Tim Stafford, "Finding the Will of God," *Marriage Partnership*, Spring 1989, p. 28.
[4]Chuck Swindoll, *The Will of God* (Portland, Ore.: Multnomah Press, 1980), pp. 3-4.

Chapter 2: Praying to Become Wise in Decision-Making
[1]James Dobson, *Emotions: Can You Trust Them?* (Ventura, Calif.: Regal, 1980), p. 118.
[2]Thomas Bertram Costain, *The Silver Chalice* (Garden City, N.Y.: Doubleday, 1952), p. 177.

Chapter 3: The Role of the Holy Spirit in Guidance
[1]Dick Eastman, *Change the World School of Prayer* (N.p.: World Literature Crusade, 1976), pp. 197-98.
[2]John Sullivan,"God, Send Someone," *Guideposts*, November 1955, pp. 1-5.
[3]George Mallone, *Those Miraculous Gifts* (Downers Grove, Ill.: InterVarsity Press, 1983), p. 63.
[4]For more about this topic, see J. E. O'Day's helpful booklet *Discovering Your Spiritual Gifts* (Downers Grove, Ill.: InterVarsity Press, 1985).
[5]Kermit A. Echlebarger, "Are We Fleecing Ourselves?" *Moody Monthly*, November 1984, pp. 27-28.
[6]Dan Beltzer, "Providence," *Leadership* 12, no. 3 (Summer 1991): 48.

Chapter 4: Why Prayer Is Essential to Discovering God's Will
[1]Ron Dunn, *Don't Just Stand There, Pray Something* (Nashville: Thomas Nelson, 1991), pp. 21-23.
[2]Jim Petersen, *Evangelism as a Lifestyle* (Colorado Springs: NavPress, 1980), p. 142.

Chapter 5: Learning About Prayer from the Master
[1]Aleksandr Solzhenitsyn, *One Day in the Life of Ivan Denisovich* (New York: Signet, 1963), pp. 121-22.

[2]John Guest, *Finding Deeper Intimacy with God: Only a Prayer Away* (Grand Rapids, Mich.: Baker Book House, 1992), p. 116.

[3]Ron Dunn, *Don't Just Stand There, Pray Something* (Nashville: Thomas Nelson, 1991), pp. 91-92.

Chapter 6: Praying for Discernment in Dealing with the Enemy

[1]For further discussion of the battlefield of prayer, see Ron Dunn, *Don't Just Stand There, Pray Something* (Nashville: Thomas Nelson, 1991), pp. 67-70.

[2]Ralph W. Neighbour Jr., *The Shepherd's Guide Book* (Houston: Touch Outreach Ministries, 1988), p. 48.

[3]Bill Jackson, "Waging War," *World Christian*, January/February 1985, p. 11.

[4]Frank Peretti, *Piercing the Darkness* (Westchester, Ill.: Crossway, 1989), p. 80.

[5]Frank Peretti, *This Present Darkness* (Westchester, Ill.: Crossway, 1986), p. 325.

Chapter 7: The Importance of Praise in Obtaining Guidance

[1]Alan Loy McGinnis, *The Power of Optimism* (San Francisco: Harper & Row, 1990), p. 57.

[2]Ibid., p. 85.

[3]Lloyd John Ogilvie, *God's Will in Your Life* (Eugene, Ore.: Harvest House, 1982), pp. 141-43.

[4]Max Lucado, *God Came Near* (Portland, Ore.: Multnomah Press, 1987), pp. 13-14.

[5]Dietrich Bonhoeffer, *Life Together* (New York: Harper & Row, 1954), p. 29.

Chapter 8: The Necessity of Confession in Obtaining Guidance

[1]Lloyd H. Steffen, "Confession," *Leadership* 12, no. 2 (Spring 1991): 45.

Chapter 9: Praying for God's Will in Healing

[1]David Wang, "Testimonies from Around the World," *Christian Life*, October 1982, p. 53.

[2]Paul Eshleman, *I Just Saw Jesus* (Laguna Niguel, Calif.: Jesus Project, 1985), p. 110.

[3]Billy Graham, *The Holy Spirit* (Waco, Tex.: Word, 1978), p. 241.

[4]Kyle Duncan and Carol Jackson, "God's Quiet Servant," *Focus on the Family*, June 1989, p. 16.

Chapter 10: Praying with Faith

[1]Ian Gunn-Russel, "Everything Possible?" *Guideposts*, July 1989, pp. 38-40.

[2]Richard Doebler, "Ambassador for an Inscrutable God," *Leadership* 12, no. 3 (Summer 1991): 29.

[3]Timothy M. Warner, "Encounter with Demon Power," *Trinity World Forum*, Winter 1981, p. 3.

Chapter 11: Praying to Discern God's Will for a Group Decision

[1]I am indebted to Norman Shawchuck, who first acquainted me with some of these group discernment principles during a course at Trinity Evangelical Divinity School.

Chapter 12: The Importance of Praying in Jesus' Name

[1]John Steinbeck, *East of Eden* (New York: Viking, 1952).

[2]John Guest, *Finding Deeper Intimacy with God* (Grand Rapids, Mich.: Baker Book House, 1992), pp. 36-37.